Julie Hegedus

ISBN 1-930596-35-9

Published by THE GUEST COTTAGE, INC.
PO Box 848
Woodruff, WI 54568
1-800-333-8122
www.theguestcottage.com

Designed and marketed by The Guest Cottage Inc.
Cover art by Julie Hegedus

Printed in U.S.A.

Celebrate Breakfast!

A Cookbook & Travel Guide

Recipes from the

Innkeepers of the Michigan Lake to Lake

Bed & Breakfast Association

Acknowledgments

Thank you to all involved in producing this beautiful cookbook/travel guide. It would not have happened without the dedication, persistence, and patience of the participating Michigan Lake to Lake B&B Association members.

Thank you to the creative staff at Guest Cottage for your support. And thanks also to artist Julie Hegedus of Whitehall, Michigan for the wonderful artwork for the cover.

For more information about Michigan Lake to Lake Bed & Breakfast Association, please visit our website at: http://www.laketolake.com

Contents

Participating Inns

State Map of Participating Inns

Guide By City of Participating Inns

Castle in the Country

340 M-40 Highway South
Allegan, MI 49010
(269)673-8054
(888)673-8054
www.castleinthecountry.com
info@castleinthecountry.com

Hosts: Herb & Ruth Boven

Come on out to the country, where enchantment, adventure and romance meet… and memories are made to last forever!

We have two extraordinary buildings, one a classic three-story Victorian, called the Castle, and one a more contemporary, newly remodeled masterpiece, called the Castle Keep. Both are wrapped in our 65 acres with gazebo, gardens, screened house with dock at a private lake, and walking trails into our enchanted forest. Relax on the wraparound porch or brick patio with fountain, or just take in the abundance of beautiful landscapes in every direction and in every season.

Choose from our seven spacious whirlpool/fireplace suites, all featuring king or queen size beds and separate showers, several with two-person showers. Or choose our intimate under the eaves or in the turret third floor rooms in our Victorian Castle or the luxurious first floor Camelot's Chambers in the Castle Keep. Beautiful décor with rich details envelop you in warmth and comfort.

Gourmet breakfasts are served daily, with your choice of service: in-suite, alfresco on the deck, or in one of our dining rooms overlooking the pond. We treat you royally with Friday evening appetizer gatherings, wine tasting and murder mystery dinners. We also have romantic picnic baskets stuffed with freshly baked breads, crackers, cheese and fruit, and featuring locally made wine or sparkling juice.

Rates at Castle in the Country range from $115 to $225.
Rates include a full breakfast.

Honey-baked Shrimp

Need an elegant, yet simple recipe for your next gathering? Try this appetizer that is sure to get rave reviews from all of your guests!

Makes 8-10 appetizers

1 pound shrimp, peeled and de-veined
1/2 cup olive oil
1 Tablespoon soy sauce
1 Tablespoon Cajun seasoning (dry)
2 Tablespoons honey
3 Tablespoons chopped fresh parsley, divided
1 Tablespoon lemon juice
1 lemon, cut into wedges
1 loaf crusty French bread

baking sheet with rim
1 medium mixing bowl
platter with small bowl for serving

Baking Time: 10 minutes
Baking Temperature: 400°

In a medium mixing bowl, combine olive oil, soy sauce, Cajun seasoning, lemon juice, honey and 1 Tablespoon parsley. Add shrimp. Marinate in the refrigerator for 1 hour.

Preheat oven to 400°. Place shrimp, with marinating liquid, on rimmed baking sheet. Bake for 10 minutes, until shrimp turns opaque.

Serve on a platter topped with remaining parsley and lemon wedges. Pour baked marinating liquid into small bowl and serve with sliced French bread.

Saravilla Bed & Breakfast

633 North State Street
Alma, MI 48801
(989)463-4078
www.saravilla.com
Ljdarrow@saravilla.com

Hosts: Linda & Jon Darrow

If you are interested in historic and unique, have we got a Bed & Breakfast for you! Our 11,000 square foot mansion, full of original features, was built in 1894 as a summer cottage for a very self-indulged young woman. We are centrally located in the lower peninsula and on the way to everywhere! You can enjoy wood-burning fireplaces, whirlpools, ping-pong, billiards and a hot tub. Or you can relax on our wrap-around front porch or stroll in our English garden with pond. We are only 2 blocks from downtown and 18 miles from Michigan's largest casino.

Rates at Saravilla Bed & Breakfast range from $90 to $155.
Rates include a full breakfast.

Apple Cinnamon Crescents

Just right in two bites! A light, tasty, fruit-filled treat!

Serves 8

1 can refrigerated crescent rolls (Pillsbury brand is best)
2 Tablespoons margarine, melted
2 large Golden Delicious apples —peeled, cored and cut into 8 wedges
1/4 cup sugar
1/2 teaspoon cinnamon
1/4 cup orange juice

1 small mixing bowl
9" x 13" baking pan (preferably glass)

Baking Time: 30-35 minutes
Baking Temperature: 400°

Preheat oven to 400°. Mix together sugar and cinnamon in small mixing bowl; set aside. Unroll crescent roll dough; separate into 8 rectangles. Cut each rectangle in half lengthwise to make 16 triangular strips.

Place an apple wedge on the wide end of each strip and roll up. Arrange rolls in a baking dish. Drizzle with melted margarine. Sprinkle with sugar-cinnamon mixture. Pour orange juice around, not over, the rolls.

Bake for 30-35 minutes or until rolls are golden brown and apple wedges are tender. Serve warm.

Another great recipe from Saravilla Bed & Breakfast:

Banana Yogurt Bread

This is a great way to use up those soft bananas that can't be served otherwise. This bread is especially good when it's fresh. The recipe makes two loaves, so you can serve one and freeze the other one for those times when you're too busy to bake or it's too hot to bake. It's great with or without nuts. Serve with butter or cream cheese for an added treat.

Serves 10

3/4 cup margarine
1/2 cup white sugar
3 large eggs
3-1/2 cups all-purpose flour
1 Tablespoon baking powder
1 teaspoon baking soda
1 teaspoon salt
2 Tablespoons lemon juice
4 large, very ripe bananas
3/4 cup plain yogurt or buttermilk

2 9"x5"x3" bread pans
2 large mixing bowls
1 small mixing bowl
electric mixer (works best)
spatula
masher (fork works just as well)
cooling rack(s)

Baking Time: 50-60 minutes
Baking Temperature: 350°

Preheat oven to 350°. In a large mixing bowl, sift flour, baking powder, baking soda and salt together; set aside. In a small mixing bowl, combine bananas and lemon juice; mash into a smooth paste. In another large mixing bowl, cream margarine and sugar. Add eggs, one at a time, to creamed mixture, beating well after each addition.

Add flour mixture to creamed mixture. Fold in banana mixture. Pour batter into greased and floured loaf pans. Smooth batter evenly in pans, making sure batter is spread up the edges of the pan.

Bake for 50-60 minutes or until wooden toothpick inserted in center comes out clean. Cool in pans no longer than 10 minutes. Remove from pans and cool completely on wire racks.

Another great recipe from Saravilla Bed & Breakfast:

Pecan Crescent Rolls

What smells better than a cinnamon roll fresh out of the oven! These mini cinnamon rolls are very easy and very good – everyone likes them. Each one is only two bites but just the right size to satisfy that sweet tooth without feeling like you overdid it!

Serves 8

1 can (8 ounces) crescent rolls
4 ounces cream cheese, softened
1/4 cup white sugar
1/2 teaspoon cinnamon
1/2 teaspoon vanilla
1/4 cup finely chopped pecans

baking sheet
1 small mixing bowl
spatula
serrated knife

Baking Time: 11-15 minutes
Baking Temperature: 375°

Preheat oven to 375°. In a small mixing bowl, blend cream cheese, sugar, cinnamon and vanilla until smooth. Stir in pecans.

Separate crescent rolls into 4 rectangles; firmly press perforations to seal. Spread about 2 Tablespoons of cream cheese mixture over each rectangle to within 1/4 inch of edges. Starting at shortest side, roll up; pinch seams to seal. Cut into 4 slices. Place cut-side down on ungreased baking sheet.

Bake for 11-15 minutes or until golden brown.

Glaze:
1/2 cup powdered sugar
2-3 teaspoons milk

In a small mixing bowl, blend ingredients until smooth – glaze needs to be stiff. Place a dab on top of each roll before serving.

Ann Arbor Bed & Breakfast

921 East Huron Street
Ann Arbor, MI 48104
(734)994-9100
www.annarborbedandbreakfast.com
pat@annarborbedandbreakfast.com

Hosts: Bob & Pat Materka

Overlooking the University of Michigan's central campus, the Ann Arbor Bed and Breakfast offers business and leisure travelers hospitality, convenience and comfort. U-M theaters, auditoriums and conference centers are across the street. Shops, galleries and museums on campus and downtown are within easy walking distance.

With its Swiss chalet roof, glass front cathedral ceilings, wrap-around balconies and sunken living room, the 1962 home is a classic example of mid-century modern architecture. It features nine individually themed bedrooms, each with private baths, TV/DVDs, high speed internet and whimsical, eclectic décor. You can count stars through the skylights of Maine Woods, cozy into a hand-hewn log bed in Yellowstone, or sleep under a breaking wave in Laguna Beach.

At breakfast, you are likely to meet visitors from around the globe, ranging from visiting lecturers and researchers, professionals attending meetings and conferences, to alumni returning for a reunion or sports event, or parents bringing students for a campus tour.

Visitors are drawn not only to the University but to Ann Arbor itself, a vibrant, engaging city known for its annual Art Fair, Summer Festival, Film Festival, the Rolling Sculpture Car Show and numerous other special events.

Rates at Ann Arbor Bed & Breakfast range from $129 to $159.
Rates include a full breakfast.

Versatile Make-ahead Crepes

Crepes are a mainstay of our Bed & Breakfast menu. A benefit of crepes is that you can whip up a large quantity, fill them the night before for easy morning heating, and refrigerate or freeze the extras for future use. Adding minced fresh spinach (or parsley or other herbs) to the batter creates a surprising, attractive design on the finished pancake.

Serves 4-5

1-1/4 cups flour
pinch of salt
1 large egg, slightly beaten
1-1/4 cups milk
1 Tablespoon melted butter or vegetable oil

light olive oil, spray vegetable oil, or melted butter to grease pan

crepe pan (recommended) or shallow 10" skillet
1 medium mixing bowl
blender, electric mixer, or whisk
baking pan *(10" x 10" x 2" or size needed to accommodate rolled crepes)*

Baking Time: 20 minutes
Baking Temperature: 350°

In a medium mixing bowl, blend flour and salt. Make a well in the center of the dry ingredients and pour in liquid ingredients. Using a blender, electric mixer or whisk, mix all ingredients; smooth out any lumps, but do not over beat. Allow batter to rest covered for 30 minutes at room temperature. Batter can be refrigerated for up to 2 days. The final mixture is a batter with the consistency of heavy cream. Have fun and experiment. Add water if batter is too thick; add a bit of flour if it's too thin.

To cook, put a little butter or oil in a nonstick crepe pan or heavy seasoned skillet. The pan is hot enough when it smokes and a sprinkle of water forms beads and evaporates. Pour off excess oil. Ladle about 1/3 cup batter into pan and swish it around, tilting pan until it's coated with a thin layer of batter. On medium high heat, cook 1-2 minutes or until top is set and bottom is light golden. Flip with spatula and cook for 30-45 seconds. Remove to wax paper. Repeat, lightly buttering pan before each new crepe.

Stack the finished crepes between sheets of wax paper. They can be stored for up to 3 days in the refrigerator or up to 1 month in the freezer.

Variations:
-Add finely chopped spinach, parsley, herbs or all of these to the batter to add color and interest.
-Substitute buckwheat or whole wheat flour for white flour, or mix. Add 2 extra eggs and allow 1 hour to rest.

Fillings:
For savory crepes, any combination of sautéed vegetables and grated cheese. Meat is optional.
Some examples include:
-Asparagus, ham and Gruyere cheese
-Spinach, bacon, tomato and Cheddar cheese
-Roasted red peppers and goat cheese
-Mushrooms, peppers and Monterey Jack cheese
-Broccoli, chicken, mushrooms and Havarti cheese
-Smoked salmon and Crème Fraiche (serve at room temperature-do not bake)

Preheat oven to 350°. I usually put a spoonful of filling in the crepe center and fold it like a package. Place crepes seam-side down in a baking dish and top with grated cheese. Bake uncovered for 20 minutes. If the dish has been refrigerated, bake for 20 minutes covered and 10 minutes more uncovered.

Another great recipe from Ann Arbor Bed & Breakfast:

Fresh Tomato Basil Tart

Baked in a shallow pie pan or individual tart pans, this dish is a tasty and colorful accompaniment or alternative to a classic egg quiche. Prepare the crust and filling a day ahead and bake in the morning – or bake it all the night before and serve at room temperature.

Serves 8-10

Pastry:
- **2 cups flour**
- **1/2 teaspoon salt**
- **2 teaspoons baking powder**
- **1/2 cup (1 stick) unsalted butter, chilled and cut into small pieces**
- **2/3 cup whole milk**

Filling:
- **3 pounds ripe tomatoes, diced into 1/2 inch chunks**
- **2 Tablespoons chopped fresh basil**
- **3 Tablespoons chopped fresh chives**
- **3/4 teaspoon salt**
- **1/4 pound sharp White Cheddar Cheese, grated, divided**
- **2/3 cup mayonnaise**

2 shallow 8-inch or 9-inch pie pans or 12 tart pans
pastry blender
2 medium mixing bowls

Baking Time: 27-28 minutes, divided
Baking Temperature: 400°

Preheat oven to 400°. Prepare the pastry by sifting dry ingredients together, then cutting in butter with a pastry blender or 2 knives, until the butter resembles small peas. Stir in milk. Knead slightly and roll out on floured board. Divide in half to line pie pans or pat evenly into small tart pans. Bake crusts until golden brown, about 7-8 minutes.

Prepare the filling by reserving half the cheese, then mixing remaining ingredients together in medium mixing bowl. Spoon evenly into pie shells or tart pans. Sprinkle reserved cheese evenly on top. Bake until golden brown, about 20 minutes.

Serve warm or at room temperature.

Another great recipe from Ann Arbor Bed & Breakfast:

Asparagus Pepper Quiche

This easy, attractive quiche can be assembled the night before and baked in the morning, or made ahead and reheated. It can be served warm or at room temperature and works well for breakfasts served buffet style. Omit the bacon (or sprinkle on half the pie) for a vegetarian option.

Serves 8-10

1 prepared pastry sheet (or your from-scratch recipe)
3 cups shredded cheese (Gruyere, Gouda, Sharp Cheddar or Monterey Jack are good choices)
12 6-inch asparagus spears plus 3 cups additional chopped asparagus, uncooked
6 eggs
1-1/2 cups heavy cream or half-and-half
1 cup cooked, crumbled bacon, optional
1 cup chopped parsley, optional
1 cup diced red, orange and yellow peppers, optional
seasoning to taste

11.5-inch ceramic quiche pan (recommended) or large pie pan
1 medium mixing bowl
whisk

Baking Time: 37-38 minutes, divided
Baking Temperature: 400°

Preheat oven to 400°. Line quiche pan with pastry; bake 7-8 minutes or until light brown.

Evenly sprinkle shredded cheese and chopped asparagus. In a medium mixing bowl, beat eggs, cream and seasoning together; pour into pan. Sprinkle more cheese, bacon, parsley and peppers, if desired. Arrange asparagus in pinwheel on top.

Bake for 30 minutes or until filling is set.

Variations: Add 1 to 2 cups sautéed mushrooms, broccoli sprigs, diced fresh tomatoes, or fresh baby spinach leaves – or a combination of whatever fresh vegetables you have on hand.

Arcadia House Bed & Breakfast

17304 Sixth Street (Scenic M-22)
Arcadia, MI 49613
(231)889-4394
www.thearcadiahouse.com
info@thearcadiahouse.com

Hosts: Greg & Patrice Wisner

Our lovely 1910 historic home in the lakeshore village of Arcadia was the long time residence of Charles P. Matteson, who operated the general store next door. Careful restoration has preserved the home's Edwardian elegance and added modern comfort and convenience. Amenities include central air conditioning, on-site massage therapist, outdoor garden, spa/Jacuzzi and parlor room with fireplace. We have five guest rooms, each with their own private bath.

Arcadia (peaceful) is nestled in a lovely valley between high, wooded bluffs, presenting spectacular views of Lake Michigan. Arcadia House is a wonderful place to relax, where our guests can enjoy unspoiled beaches, world class golf, tennis, birding, hiking, biking, snow sports and more!

Rates at Arcadia House Bed & Breakfast range from $99 to $119.
Rates include a full breakfast.

Savannah Pecan and Banana Pancakes

Our guests just love these wonderful, comforting pancakes. They say that the texture and presentation is the best that they have ever had. We proudly serve them with fresh strawberries and real maple syrup grown and made locally. A great start to your vacation day!

Serves 4-6

1 cup all-purpose flour
1 cup whole wheat flour
2 Tablespoons sugar
2 teaspoons baking powder
1/2 teaspoon salt
1-1/2 cups buttermilk (or 1-1/2 Tablespoons lemon juice and enough milk to make 1-1/2 cups—allow to sit for a few minutes)
1/4 cup vegetable oil
2 large eggs
1 cup (about 1-1/2 medium-large) yellow bananas, thinly sliced
1/2 cup toasted chopped pecans (cooled)

Garnishes:
powdered sugar
banana slices
toasted pecan halves
fresh strawberry slices
real maple syrup

measuring cups and spoons
toaster oven or microwave to toast pecans
1 medium mixing bowl
1 large mixing bowl
scraper/spatula for folding
electric griddle or skillet
ladle
large pancake spatula for turning

Combine flours, sugar, baking powder, and salt in a medium mixing bowl. Set aside. In a large mixing bowl, beat together buttermilk, oil and eggs until well blended. Slowly blend flour mixture into egg mixture until smooth. Do not overbeat. Fold in bananas and pecans.

Heat a lightly greased (vegetable oil) griddle or skillet to medium high heat (approx. 400°-425°) or until a few drops of water dance on the surface. Ladle 1/4 cup of the batter onto the hot griddle. Cook 2-3 minutes or until the top is covered with bubbles and edges look dry. Turn the pancakes and cook for an additional 2 minutes or until the undersides are brown. (Do not flip again.)

Lightly dust with powdered sugar. Garnish on top with a few additional sliced bananas, toasted pecan halves and fresh strawberry slices. Serve warm with real maple syrup. Yummy!

Grand Victorian Bed & Breakfast

402 North Bridge Street
P.O. Box 312
Bellaire, MI 49615
(231)533-6111
(877)438-6111
www.grandvictorian.com
innkeeper@grandvictorian.com

Hosts: Ken & Linda Fedraw

The Grand Victorian is centrally located in Northern Michigan's famed Chain O'Lakes. Every effort has been made to ensure that your stay at the Inn is one you'll remember for a long, long time. This Queen Anne Victorian was built in 1895 by Henry Richardi, then owner of a wooden works factory close by. Immediately upon entering the home, you will be taken back to a time of one hundred-year-old craftsmanship and absorb the ambiance of a hand-carved oak staircase, chestnut parlor, ornate chandeliers, hand-carved fireplaces and a drawing room of exquisite bird's-eye maple with bay windows surrounded in etched glass. The home is listed on the U.S. Dept. of Interior's List of Historical Places, its picture has graced the cover of Midwest Living, Traverse and Country Inns magazines, numerous calendars, and several breakfast promotions by Nabisco®, Pepperidge Farms®, and Land O Lakes®.

Rates at Grand Victorian Bed & Breakfast range from $95 to $195.
Rates include a full gourmet breakfast.

Fudgy Caramel Delight

Doesn't the name just say it all¿¿

Makes 16-20 squares

Bottom Layer:
1 cup (8 ounces) milk chocolate chips
1/4 cup butterscotch chips
1/4 cup creamy peanut butter

Filling:
1/4 cup butter
1 cup sugar
1/4 cup evaporated milk
1 jar (7 ounces) marshmallow crème
1/4 cup creamy peanut butter
1 teaspoon vanilla
1-1/2 cups lightly salted peanuts, chopped

Caramel Layer:
1 package (14 ounces) caramels
1/4 cup heavy or whipping cream

Icing:
1 cup (8 ounces) milk chocolate chips
1/4 cup butterscotch chips
1/4 cup creamy peanut butter

9" x 13" pan
2-quart glass measuring container
heavy saucepan

For bottom layer, combine the three ingredients in a 2-quart measuring container and microwave the chips and peanut butter until melted, about 1-1/2 minutes. Stir until smooth. Spread onto the bottom of a lightly greased pan. Refrigerate until set. For filling, melt butter in a heavy saucepan over med-high heat. Add sugar and milk. Bring to a boil; boil and stir for 5 minutes. Remove from heat; stir in the marshmallow crème, peanut butter and vanilla. Add peanuts. Spread over first layer. Refrigerate until set.

Combine caramels and cream in 2-quart glass measuring container. Microwave for 1-1/2 minutes or until melted and smooth. Stir well to make sure it's thoroughly melted. If necessary, microwave for another 30 seconds. Spread over the filling. Refrigerate until set. For the icing, combine ingredients in a 2-quart measuring container and microwave until melted, about 1-1/2 minutes. Stir until smooth and pour over the caramel layer.

Refrigerate for at least 1 hour. Cut into squares. Store in refrigerator.

The Inn at the Rustic Gate

6991 Hungerford Lake Drive
Big Rapids, MI 49307
(231)976-2328
(800)319-5867
www.innattherusticgate.com
innattherusticgate@starband.net

Hosts: Patricia Barrett, Marcia Stroko, and Sharon Stroko

The Inn at the Rustic Gate is a welcoming, calm place that invites guests to step back from the demands of everyday life. There is room to roam on the Inn's 146 acres, complete with lake and pond. Meeting space, picnic pavilion, library and Meditation Loft provide individuals and groups with a peaceful setting. Our Inn is especially suited to host retreats, workshops, conferences, club meetings and special events. Gourmet breakfast is included. Our resident chef can provide other meals upon request.

Rates at The Inn at the Rustic Gate range from $100 to $135.
Rates include a full breakfast.

"I can't believe I just ate Prune Muffins"

Whenever I serve these muffins to our guests, I always tell them that they are a fruit and nut muffin with a secret ingredient. I challenge them to guess the secret, but no one has yet been correct. When I reveal that the fruit is actually cherry essence prunes, time and time again the guests exclaim, "I can't believe I just ate prune muffins!" This is my most requested muffin recipe.

Makes 12 muffins

Nonstick vegetable oil cooking spray
1 cup Sunsweet Cherry Essence Dried Plums, chopped into small pieces
1-1/2 cups all-purpose flour
1 teaspoon baking powder
1 teaspoon baking soda
1/4 teaspoon salt
1 teaspoon cinnamon
1 large egg
1/4 cup canola oil
1/2 cup sugar
1 teaspoon vanilla extract
1 teaspoon almond extract
2/3 cup low fat sour cream
1/2 cup chopped walnuts

Topping:
2 Tablespoons sugar
1 teaspoon cinnamon
Mix sugar with cinnamon and lightly sprinkle on top of muffin batter in pan prior to baking.

Muffin pan
Knife and cutting board
Measuring cups and spoons
1 small mixing bowl and 1 medium mixing bowl
Whisk

Baking Time: 20-25 minutes
Baking Temperature: 350°

Preheat oven to 350°. Lightly coat muffin pan with nonstick cooking spray. Chop dried plums and set aside. In a small mixing bowl, sift together flour, baking powder, baking soda, salt and cinnamon. In a medium mixing bowl, hand whisk together egg, oil, sugar, vanilla and almond extracts and sour cream until blended. Fold in flour mixture until batter is just moistened. Add chopped plums and walnuts to batter.

Spoon batter into prepared muffin pan. Sprinkle top of batter with sugar/cinnamon mixture as directed above. Bake for 20-25 minutes or until golden brown. Let muffins cool in pan for 5 minutes, then remove to cool on rack.

When these muffins are served warm on the side of fresh fruit covered with vanilla yogurt and home baked granola, it makes a delicious and healthy start to the day!

Dewey Lake Manor Bed & Breakfast

11811 Laird Road
Brooklyn, MI 49230
(517)467-7122
www.deweylakemanor.com
deweylk@frontiernet.net

Hosts: Joe & Barb Phillips

Sitting atop a knoll overlooking Dewey Lake, a country retreat awaits Manor guests in the Irish Hills of southern Michigan. This Italianate-style house was built in the late 1860's by A. F. Dewey, one of five brothers whose father came west as a surveyor. Mr. Dewey was a prosperous farmer in the area who owned the lake and all the land around it. The Irish Hills is a jewel nestled among clear blue lakes, red barns, gently rolling countryside, and quaint towns. This century-old home, furnished with antiques and original kerosene chandeliers, has five guest rooms, each with queen-size bed and fireplace, one with a Jacuzzi. A large deck and glass-enclosed porch provide a pleasant place to enjoy a full breakfast or to just relax. Guests may enjoy the canoe, paddleboats, picnics, and bonfires by the lake. And don't forget to check our website for virtual tours, specials, and packages. Nearby are fine dining, wineries, antiques, and golf.

Rates at Dewey Lake Manor Bed & Breakfast range from $75 to $135.
Rates include a full breakfast.

Dewey Lake Bread Pudding

Since bread pudding is a traditional Irish dessert—and we are in the "Irish Hills"—I wanted a unique and good tasting pudding, and this is it. I use it for breakfast as well as a dessert for a regular meal—great with Irish stew.

Serves 8-10

4-6 large stale croissants
1/2 cup dried cherries or cranberries
1/2 cup golden raisins
5 large eggs
2 egg yolks
2 cups milk
3 cups half-and-half cream
1-1/2 cups white sugar
1-1/2 teaspoons vanilla

9" x 13" glass baking pan
1 large mixing bowl
whisk or electric mixer
10" x 15" pan for hot water

Baking Time: 1-1/2 hours total
Baking Temperature: 350°

Preheat oven to 350°. Grease glass baking pan. Slice croissants in half and put bottoms in greased pan. (They should fit together like a puzzle.) Place dried fruit on top of croissants. Place croissant tops over dried fruit.

Beat together eggs, milk, half-and-half, sugar and vanilla in large mixing bowl. Pour mixture over croissants. Press croissants down and soak for 15 minutes.

Place baking pan in the 10" x 15" pan filled with hot water. Cover both pans with tent of aluminum foil. Bake for 45 minutes. Remove aluminum foil. Bake for an additional 40-45 minutes.

Spoon into bowls or cut into squares. Serve with a lemon sauce or rum sauce of your choice.

The Torch Lake Bed & Breakfast, LLC

4417 Trillium Ridge Road
Central Lake, MI 49622
(231)599-3400
www.torchlakebb.com
info@torchlakebb.com

Host: Deb Cannon

Relax and be pampered! Enjoy Torch Lake the way you've always dreamed it would be. This spacious and charming Majestic Queen provides a spectacular view, sitting high above beautiful Torch Lake, listed by National Geographic as being the third most beautiful lake in the world. We are centrally located between Traverse City and Petoskey. Visit for a night or a fortnight. Relax in front of the 20-foot stone fireplace. Star gaze from the outdoor hot tub. In the morning, start your day with a tantalizing full breakfast. Your master suite will include a private bath, private deck, and king-size bed with designer sheets. Television with CD, DVD player and cable are provided in your room and in the sunroom. Refrigerator, iron and ironing board are also provided.

Please allow The Torch Lake Bed & Breakfast the opportunity to help you discover your own special place for relaxing and rejuvenating.

Rates at The Torch Lake Bed & Breakfast range from $135 to $150.
Rates include a full breakfast.

The Torch Lake Almond Chocolate Bliss

To awaken in the morning to the aroma of this absolutely delicious morning coffee cake is a perfect way to start the day. Chocolate Heaven! This coffee cake is wonderful eaten hot out of the oven or warmed back up in the microwave.

Serves 12

1-1/2 cups all-purpose flour
1/2 cup soft wheat flour
2/3 cup unsweetened cocoa powder
1/4 cup Nestle Toll House milk chocolate morsels
1 teaspoon baking soda
1 teaspoon baking powder
1/2 teaspoon salt
1/2 cup unsalted butter, softened
1 cup sugar
3 large eggs
1-1/4 cups sour cream
2 Tablespoons Miracle Whip, light or regular
1-1/2 teaspoons vanilla

2 medium mixing bowls
mixer
9" x 13" baking pan
food processor

Baking Time: 45-50 minutes
Baking Temperature: 325°

Preheat oven to 325°. In a medium mixing bowl, mix together all-purpose flour, wheat flour, cocoa, milk chocolate morsels, baking soda, baking powder and salt. In a separate bowl, cream together, with a mixer, softened butter, sugar, eggs, sour cream, Miracle Whip and vanilla. Add dry ingredients to liquid ingredients and beat on low speed for about 2 minutes or until mixture is smooth. Pour mixture into a greased and floured baking pan. Sprinkle on topping and bake for 45-50 minutes or until toothpick comes out clean.

Topping:
1 cup all-purpose flour
3/4 cup light brown sugar, packed firm
1/3 cup sliced almonds
1/2 teaspoon cinnamon
8 Tablespoons cold unsalted butter
3/4 cup Nestle Toll House milk chocolate morsels

In food processor, add flour, brown sugar, cinnamon and cold butter. Process together until mixture is crumbly. Then stir in milk chocolate morsels and almonds. Sprinkle on top of cake mixture and bake as directed above.

Waterloo Gardens Bed & Breakfast

7600 Werkner Road
Chelsea, MI 48118
(734)433-1612
(877)433-1612
www.waterloogardensbb.com
waterloogardens@prodigy.net

Hosts: Lourdean & Gary Offenbacher

Come and enjoy our large country ranch in Chelsea. We are just minutes from downtown Chelsea and Ann Arbor. While you're here, catch a performance at the world renowned Purple Rose Theatre or enjoy a gourmet meal at the Common Grill. Stroll the lovely gardens or relax on the deck. Let the master spa's heated jets melt away the stresses of the week. Play a game of pool or watch a video or DVD on the big screen television. Work out in the fitness center or read a book. There are lots of open common areas and plenty of hiking trails nearby.

Just relax and hang out.

Rates at Waterloo Gardens Bed & Breakfast range from $85 to $135.
Rates include a full breakfast.

Waterloo Gardens Apple Cake

This is a wonderful cake to serve anytime. I use a combination of apples (Red Delicious, Northern Spy and MacIntosh). My family and guests really enjoy this cake!

Serves 8-12

1 cup chopped walnuts or pecans
6 medium apples – cored, pared and thinly sliced
1 Tablespoon orange zest
2 cups plus 6 Tablespoons sugar, divided
1-1/2 teaspoons cinnamon
1 cup butter, softened
4 eggs
2-1/2 teaspoons vanilla
1/3 cup orange juice
3 cups flour
1 Tablespoon baking powder

2 large mixing bowls
electric mixer
tube pan

Baking Time: 95 minutes
Baking Temperature: 350°

Preheat oven to 350°. In a large mixing bowl, mix nuts, apples, orange zest, 6 Tablespoons sugar and cinnamon. In another large mixing bowl, combine butter, 2 cups sugar, eggs, vanilla and orange juice. Beat until fluffy. Fold in flour and baking powder to egg mixture.

Place half of the egg mixture into tube pan. Place half of the apple mixture next. Layer remaining egg mixture next. The remaining apple mixture will be the final layer. Bake for 95 minutes and let cool completely before removing from pan.

Gould Farm Bed & Breakfast Inn

8300 East Mannsiding Road
Clare, MI 48617
(989)386-3594
www.gouldfarmbandbinn.net
gouldfarm@hotmail.com

Hosts: Lynn & Judy Gould

Sitting atop a hill overlooking the farm, warm hospitality greets guests at the Gould Farm Bed & Breakfast Inn. The owners, Lynn and Judy Gould, manage a 500 head cattle operation. The traditional style farmhouse was built in 2001. It has 4 guest bedrooms that are furnished with traditional and antique furniture. The farmhouse is a quiet, peaceful place to enjoy the sounds of the country, to watch cattle graze and to see wildlife.

There is a golf course and ski resort close by plus antique shops, flea market, a large Amish community, cross country skiing, snowmobile trails, lakes and trout streams, and a large casino.

Rates at Gould Farm Bed & Breakfast Inn range from $85 to $95.
Rates include a full breakfast.

Impossible Brunch Pie

Each time we make this breakfast pie our guests tell us how delicious it is. A nice dish when fresh asparagus is available. It is easy to make and very tasty!

Serves 6-8

10 ounces asparagus spears, cooked and drained
1 cup sour cream
1 cup cottage cheese
1/2 cup Bisquick baking mix
1/4 cup melted butter or oleo
2 eggs
1 tomato, peeled and thinly sliced
1/4 cup Parmesan cheese

1 medium mixing bowl
blender or hand beater
9" pie plate

Baking Time: 30-40 minutes
Baking Temperature: 350°

Preheat oven to 350°. Put cooked asparagus in bottom of greased pie plate. In a medium mixing bowl, beat sour cream, cottage cheese, Bisquick mix, butter and eggs until smooth—15 seconds in a blender or 1 minute with a hand beater. Pour mixture over asparagus. Top with sliced tomato. Sprinkle with Parmesan cheese.

Bake for 30-40 minutes or until knife inserted in center comes out clean. Cool 5 minutes before serving.

Buttonville Inn

3049 West Saginaw Road
Coleman, MI 48618
(989)465-9364
www.buttonvilleinn.com
info@buttonvilleinn.com

Hosts: Ron & Candy Harsh

Buttonville Inn is a classic four-square, craftsman style three-story home built in the 1920s. This beautiful county manor house overlooks the nearby hillside and meandering brook. Our traditional Bed & Breakfast will remind you of a country roadhouse with French and English country style furnishings in the commons areas.When Buttonville (now North Bradley) was a lumbering town, a hotel was built on this site before the turn of the century. Using a lot of the materials from the hotel, Frank and Edith Beamish built the house that is now our Inn. The stock market crash of 1929 prevented the Beamishes from completing the house as planned, and it was purchased by two other families before we purchased it in 1999. The newly renovated Bed & Breakfast was opened in June 2001.

Buttonville Inn is a quiet, out-of-the-way place where relaxation is the main feature, with numerous recreational activities available for those outdoor enthusiasts. The rail trail, a converted railroad track, is adjacent to the Inn and provides 36 miles of paved trail for bikers and hikers. Great shopping is located near the Inn. The wraparound porch provides a great place to curl up with a good book. Four rooms, all with private baths, are individually decorated; three rooms are on the second floor and a suite is on the third floor. The Americana Room is furnished in a red, white and blue American style. The Gardenbrook Room is a red, colorful room with a spacious sitting area. The North Forty Room has a rustic lodge look with a log bed and a nice sitting area. The Cottage Thyme Suite has a washed-white queen bed with wicker furnishings.

Buttonville Inn provides quality accommodations, offering guests a quiet respite from everyday pressures and stress.

Rates at Buttonville Inn range from $75 to $109.
Rates include a full breakfast.

Apricot Scones

This is a wonderful scone for breakfast, brunch, lunch, or afternoon tea. The secret to great scones is chilling them in the refrigerator 10 minutes before baking. These scones freeze well, but I rarely have any left to freeze!

Makes 8-10 scones

2 cups flour
1/3 cup sugar
2 teaspoons baking powder
1/2 teaspoon salt
1/4 cup chilled butter
1 large egg
1 cup whipping cream
1-1/2 teaspoons vanilla
1 cup toasted walnuts, broken
1 cup finely chopped apricots
1/2 cup white chocolate chips

2-quart mixing bowl
4-quart or larger mixing bowl
baking stone

Baking Time: 15 minutes
Baking Temperature: 375°

Preheat oven to 375°. In larger mixing bowl, stir together flour, sugar, baking powder and salt. Cut in butter. In the smaller mixing bowl, mix together egg, cream and vanilla. Add cream mixture to flour mixture and knead until thoroughly combined. Knead in walnuts, apricots and white chocolate chips.

Pat dough on to a lightly floured surface until it is about 5/8-inch thick; I do this on a baking stone. Cut into 8-10 pie-shaped wedges. Refrigerate wedges for 10 minutes before baking.

Bake for 15 minutes or until lightly browned. Serve with honey butter for a special treat!

East Tawas Junction Bed & Breakfast

514 West Bay Street
East Tawas, MI 48730
(989)362-8006
www.east-tawas.com
info@east-tawas.com

Hosts: Donald & Leigh Mott

This newly redecorated, air-conditioned early 1900's country Victorian is nestled in a picturesque park-like setting overlooking beautiful Tawas Bay. The main house features 5 inviting guest rooms with private baths, feather beds, fireplaces, cable TVs, public rooms and sunny decks. The sumptuous farm fresh breakfasts are geared to get you off to a running start to enjoy the many festivals, concerts, theatre, Tawas Bay State Park Lighthouse and scenic surroundings of Northeastern Michigan's sunrise side. We're just a hop and a skip across to the sugar sand beach and park. Elegant shops & restaurants plus a two-screen theatre and harbor are within a few blocks. Bird watching, biking, golfing, canoeing, cross-country skiing and snowmobiling are among the many varied activities. The fully equipped "Chickadee Guesthouse" accommodates seven with two bedrooms and sleeping porch.

Rates at East Tawas Junction Bed & Breakfast range from $99 to $164.
Rates include a full breakfast.

Classic Poached Eggs with Panache!

We are fortunate to live in a time when science and technology have provided us with a wealth of information about our bodies, health and physical wellbeing and the positive effect that well balanced, fresh and nutritious foods have in maintaining health, energy and a joyful spirit. The resulting interest in high protein, low-fat diets led us to develop this simple but elegant poached egg with spinach recipe, which has become a favorite and is often requested by our guests.

Serves 4

16 ounces baby leaf spinach
4 eggs
2 Tablespoons grated Asiago cheese
2-4 thinly sliced red onions
6 slices bacon (crumble 2 slices for bacon bits)
6 cherry tomatoes or tomato slices
1 teaspoon soul seasoning
1 teaspoon garlic powder
hollandaise sauce *(recipe below)*
paprika

10-inch skillet
pan for poaching eggs

Rinse pre-washed spinach, pat dry with paper towels and place in lightly oiled skillet. Sprinkle spinach with soul seasoning and garlic powder. Turn on very low heat – warm only. Do not allow to cook down.

Poach eggs. Timing depends upon your method of poaching. Make sure egg whites are completely cooked and yolks are beginning to set.

Place warm spinach on 2 serving plates (I use boat shaped individual casseroles). Place onions, bacon bits and 1 Tablespoon cheese on each plate. Carefully place poached eggs on top of spinach. Place tomatoes on one side of spinach and 2 slices of bacon on the other side.

Spoon 1 Tablespoon hollandaise sauce over each egg and sprinkle with paprika.

Hollandaise Sauce:
2 egg yolks
1/2 Tablespoon cold water
1/4 cup (1/2 stick) butter, softened to room temperature
1/8 teaspoon salt
1 Tablespoon lemon juice
pinch white pepper

1 small mixing bowl
double boiler
egg whisk or small egg beater

Beat yolks until thick and lemon colored. Beat in water. Transfer to top of double boiler set over barely simmering water. Heat and stir until warm, not hot. Add butter, 1 Tablespoon at a time, stirring continuously, incorporating it well after each addition. Cook until thick enough to coat back of spoon. Remove and stir in salt, pepper and lemon juice.

The House on the Hill Bed & Breakfast

9661 Lake Street
Ellsworth, MI 49729
(231)588-6304
www.thehouseonthehill.com
innkeeper@thehouseonthehill.com

Hosts: Cindy & Tom Tomalka

Your experience at The House on the Hill Bed & Breakfast begins with a tour of the seven spacious guest rooms, all appointed beautifully, with private baths and either a queen-size or king-size bed. The comfortable common areas of the main house and carriage house are next on the tour, including the gorgeous and expansive front veranda and the sunroom with cozy fireplace. Opportunities to explore and enjoy the property are endless. Depending upon the season, enjoy hiking or snowshoeing through the 45 acres of groomed walking trails, wander through the well-maintained, colorful gardens, or canoe or kayak on St. Clair Lake where the Inn is located. Outdoor activities abound nearby in Charlevoix, the Jordan River Valley, Petoskey, Mackinac Island, Sleeping Bear Dunes National Lakeshore, Harbor Springs and the famous Tunnel of Trees. Relax in the sunroom or on the veranda for the evening social hour before enjoying dinner at nearby Rowe or Tapawingo, both within walking distance. A restful night is followed by an outstanding full three-course breakfast with fresh foods and new conversations to enjoy. Breakfast will definitely be a highlight of your stay! Relive your stay at home by preparing fabulous meals from The House on the Hill Cookbook, available at the Inn. Your experience here can linger forever!

Rates at The House on the Hill Bed & Breakfast range from $150 to $200.
Rates include a full breakfast.

Cream Cheese Quiche

You will dazzle your guests with this easy-to-prepare quiche, one of the most requested dishes at our Inn.

Serves 6

1 unbaked pie shell
1 small red onion, chopped
1 package (8 ounces) cream cheese, cubed
8 ounces fresh mushrooms
1/2 cup roasted peppers, chopped
3 Tablespoons butter
2 Tablespoons fresh thyme, chopped
5 large eggs
3/4 cup milk
4 ounces Comte Gruyere cheese, shredded
nonstick cooking spray

9-inch pie plate
12-inch skillet
1 medium mixing bowl
hand mixer

Baking Time: 45 minutes total
Baking Temperature: 425°, then 350°

Preheat oven to 425°. Place pie shell in sprayed pie plate. Cover bottom of shell with cream cheese cut into cubes. Melt butter in skillet and sauté onion and mushrooms until soft. Add peppers and thyme to skillet and stir. Let cool, then spread over cream cheese. In a medium mixing bowl, beat eggs and milk together; pour over vegetable mixture in pie plate. Spread Comte Gruyere cheese on top.

Bake for 15 minutes, then reduce temperature to 350° for 30 minutes.

Cut into 6 wedges and serve.

Sandtown Farmhouse Bed & Breakfast

W14142 Sandtown Road
Engadine, MI 49827
(906)477-6163
www.sandtownfarmhouse.com
tom@sandtownfarmhouse.com

Hosts: Tom & Caroll Harper

Breathe deeply. Relax as you visit our 1920 farmhouse sited on 80 rolling acres. Stroll our gardens, hike the trails, and hot tub under the stars. Three spacious guest rooms with private baths are en suite. Breakfast sizzles on the wood-fired cook stove. Enjoy easy drives to Tahquamenon Falls, Pictured Rocks, and Lake Michigan. "Conveniently located in the middle of nowhere."

Rates at Sandtown Farmhouse Bed & Breakfast range from $70 to $80.
Rates include a full breakfast.

Gingerbread Scones with Maple Cream Spread

A yummy, fresh baked treat just right for breakfast or afternoon tea. Spread the scones with maple cream spread like we Yoopers do for true Northern flavor.

Serves 8

Scones:

2 cups all-purpose flour
1/3 cup firmly packed brown sugar
2 teaspoons baking powder
1/8 teaspoon baking soda
1/2 teaspoon ground ginger
1/2 teaspoon ground cinnamon
1/8 teaspoon ground cloves
1/8 teaspoon ground nutmeg
1/3 cup butter, chilled
1 large egg
3 Tablespoons molasses
1/4 cup milk
1 teaspoon vanilla extract
1/2 cup raisins or currants, optional

cookie sheet or divided scone pan
food processor
1 small mixing bowl
1 small saucepan

Baking Time: 20-25 minutes
Baking Temperature: 375°

Preheat oven to 375°. Using nonstick cooking spray, spray a 10-inch diameter circle in the center of a cookie sheet or spray a divided scone pan.

Combine flour, sugar, leavening agents and spices in work bowl of food processor. Cut chilled butter into about 5 pieces. Pulse food processor until mixture resembles coarse crumbs. Alternately, cut the butter into the flour using 2 knives in scissor fashion.

In a small mixing bowl, beat the egg; add milk, molasses and vanilla. Add egg mixture all at once to dry ingredients, stirring to combine. Dough will be sticky. Stir in raisins, if desired.

Portion dough into scone pan or, using lightly floured hands, pat the dough into an 8-inch diameter circle in the center of the baking sheet. With a knife, cut into 8 wedges. Sprinkle with coarse sugar before baking to add a special touch. Bake for 20-25 minutes.

Maple Cream Spread:
1/2 cup genuine maple syrup
6 ounces cream cheese at room temperature

Cook maple syrup in a small saucepan until a candy thermometer reads 235°. Allow syrup to cool to room temperature. Combine cream cheese and syrup.

Glen Arbor Bed & Breakfast and Cottages

6548 Western Avenue
P.O. Box 580
Glen Arbor, MI 49636
(231)334-6789
(877)253-4200
www.glenarborbnb.com
Innkeeper@glenarborbnb.com

Hosts: Jody Arendale & Brian Koppenaal

A very special corner of the world, Michigan's Leelanau Peninsula, awaits you.

Our striking 19th century Inn is in the heart of the village of Glen Arbor, surrounded by the picturesque Sleeping Bear Dunes National Lakeshore, and only steps from Lake Michigan's sugar sand beaches. Gorgeous lakes, towering sand dunes and stunning views are everywhere. There is also hiking, biking, golf, tennis, swimming, antiquing, wineries, lighthouses, canoeing, fishing, boutique shopping, fine dining and classic taverns, loads of galleries, and many picturesque corners to wander.

A stay at the Glen Arbor Bed & Breakfast and Cottages is sure to make your days on the Leelanau Peninsula unforgettable. Choose from six rooms and suites and two cottages that are filled with warm hospitality, elegant French Country furnishings, gracious amenities, and gourmet breakfasts every day. We even feature special quilters' and scrapbookers' escape weekends and unique photo tours in the spring and fall.

No wonder we were featured in Midwest Living Magazine. The directions are simple: come to the stop sign on the newly-designated Scenic Heritage Route M-22 in Glen Arbor. We're right there.

Rates at Glen Arbor Bed & Breakfast and Cottages range from $89 to $195.
Rates include a full breakfast.

Glen Arbor Honey Vanilla Granola

Make this your signature breakfast treat, too. Healthy, crunchy, and a perfect blend of flavors. Glen Arbor Honey Vanilla Granola is a hit as a cereal with milk or cream, a terrific topper for fruit or yogurt, or on pancakes or waffles. We're asked for the recipe—or a bag to take home—again and again and again.

Makes 8 cups

1/2 cup sliced almonds
4 cups uncooked oatmeal
1/2 cup shredded coconut
1/2 cup crunchy cereal nuggets, such as Grape-Nuts®
1/2 cup dry Wheatena cereal or 1/4 cup sesame seeds
1/2 cup oil
1/2 cup honey
1 Tablespoon vanilla
1/2 Tablespoon nutmeg
1/2 cup dried cherries or raisins

1 large mixing bowl *(we often use a large wooden bowl)*
1 medium mixing bowl
measuring cups and spoons
food processor or nut chopper
cookie sheet or jelly roll pan

Baking Time: 30-36 minutes
Baking Temperature: 300°

Preheat oven to 300°. Slice almonds in food processor. In a large mixing bowl, combine all dry ingredients except nutmeg and cherries or raisins. In a medium mixing bowl, mix together oil, honey and vanilla. Pour liquid mixture over dry mixture and mix thoroughly (hands are OK for this). Sprinkle nutmeg over this mixture and combine.

Spread on a cookie sheet or jelly roll pan and bake on middle rack of oven for 30-36 minutes, checking to make sure it does not become too brown.

Cool and mix in dried cherries or raisins. Place in airtight containers or bags. May easily be frozen if the granola will not be used within 3-4 days.

The Looking Glass Inn

1100 South Harbor
Grand Haven, MI 49417
(616)842-7150
(800)951-6427
www.bbonline.com/mi/lookingglass

Hosts: Howie & Norma Glass

Our three-story home offers a spectacular view from high up on the dune overlooking the Grand Haven Lighthouse, the harbor, and the beautiful beaches. All of our rooms have a view of Lake Michigan, two of them overlooking the golden sandy beaches and lighthouse from your luxurious bed. All guest rooms have been uniquely decorated and include either a king or queen size bed with private bath.

Our home offers a casual beach house atmosphere where you can relax and feel right at home! We would like to share our fantastic view, beautiful sunsets and casual hospitality with you, our special guest!

Rates at The Looking Glass Inn range from $135 to $150.
Rates include a full breakfast.

Overnight Rolls

Our favorite! Easy and delicious—the smell brings guests downstairs before breakfast is ready to serve! You can fix the night before—just bake and serve in the morning.

Makes 20 rolls

3/4 cup brown sugar
1 Tablespoon cinnamon
1 Tablespoon instant vanilla pudding
1 stick (1/2 cup) margarine
20 frozen bread rolls
nonstick cooking spray

bundt pan
saucepan
plastic wrap
serving plate

Baking Time: 20-25 minutes
Baking Temperature: 350°

Melt first 4 ingredients in saucepan—do not boil. Dip frozen rolls in mixture. Place frozen rolls in bundt pan sprayed with nonstick cooking spray. Pour any remaining mixture over rolls.

Cover pan with plastic wrap. Put in cool oven overnight to rise – do not heat oven.

In the morning, remove pan from oven and preheat oven to 350°. Uncover pan and bake for 20-25 minutes. Let cool for 10 minutes. Invert on serving plate.

Prairieside Suites Luxury Bed & Breakfast

3180 Washington Avenue Southwest
Grandville, MI 49418
(616)538-9442
www.prairiesidesuites.com
cheri@prairiesidesuites.com

Hosts: Cheri & Paul Antozak

If you like browsing Better Homes & Gardens Magazine, then you're going to love staying with us. We've combined our talents (interior design/licensed builder) to create a "Home Remodeling Showroom" where you'll experience the excitement of a home that has been totally redesigned and remodeled using the newest and latest technology, innovative ideas, plus a few surprises!

This wonderful, unique Bed & Breakfast caters to the business traveler and getaway couples. King beds, private baths, fireplaces, whirlpools, air conditioning, CD player, TV/VCR, coffeemaker/beverage center, refrigerator/microwave, cable modem, heated towel bars, phone/fax/copier...all in your room!

Enjoy our beautiful gardens, heated pool, pergola, and fountain! The elegant décor, the relaxed atmosphere, and the quiet, yet convenient location (restaurants and shopping malls only two minutes away) make this a perfect getaway. Our bedroom suites will pamper you, and you'll discover ways to enhance your own home! We've anticipated your every need. This luxury three bedroom Bed & Breakfast is open all year. Second/third night discounts are available.

Rates at Prairieside Suites Luxury Bed & Breakfast range from $125 to $185.
Rates include a full breakfast.

Zucchini Crumble (tastes just like apple...really)

We serve this mystery fruit crumble and let our guests guess what is in it. When I tell them the fruit is actually zucchini, they can't believe it! I am not surprised to hear that they loved it even when they don't usually like zucchini! What makes this recipe different is that you peel and remove the seeded core of the zucchini, then you chop the flesh into 1/2" x 1/2" pieces, and it looks, acts, and tastes like apple! The bigger the zucchini the better. A great recipe!

Serves 12-16

Topping and crust:
- **4 cups flour**
- **1/2 cup sugar**
- **1/2 teaspoon salt**
- **3 sticks (1-1/2 cups) melted butter**

Filling:
- **7 cups zucchini, peeled, seeded and chopped into 1/2" x 1/2" pieces**
- **2/3 cup lemon juice**
- **1-1/4 cups sugar or Splenda® sweetener**
- **1/2 teaspoon cinnamon**
- **3 Tablespoons tapioca**

9" x 13" pan
cutting board and knife
5-quart pan
food processor or mixer
measuring cups/spoons

Baking Time: 20-25 minutes
Baking Temperature: 375°

Preheat oven to 375°.

Topping and crust:
Mix all ingredients in food processor or mixer. Reserve 1 cup of mixture for topping; press the rest into the bottom of a 9" x 13" pan.

Filling:
In a 5-quart pan, boil zucchini and lemon juice together until tender. Add sugar, cinnamon and tapioca. Mix together and spread on crust. Crumble reserved topping over filling and bake for 20-25 minutes.

Shaded Oaks Bed & Breakfast

444 Oak Street
Holland, MI 49424
(616)399-4194
www.shadedoaks.com
shadedoaks@chartermi.net

Hosts: Jack & Karen Zibell

This charming Cape Cod offers a wooded setting in a beach neighborhood 75 feet off Lake Macatawa. Elegantly appointed common areas and spacious luxury suites include fireplaces, double tubs, lounge areas and private baths. Enjoy a gourmet breakfast then walk to beautiful Lake Michigan at the State Park. Open all year.

Rates at Shaded Oaks Bed & Breakfast range from $189 to $225.
Rates include a full breakfast.

Pumpkin Bread with Honey and Nut Cream Cheese Icing

Every year when the fall air becomes brisk, we get out our favorite pumpkin recipes. We love baking this bread in the autumn and pumpkin is one of those wonderful comfort tastes and smells!

Makes 7 small loaves or 4 medium loaves

2/3 cup shortening
2-2/3 cups sugar
4 eggs, beaten
2 cups (1 small can) pumpkin
2/3 cup water
3-1/2 cups flour
2 teaspoons baking soda
1/2 teaspoon baking powder
1-1/2 teaspoons salt
1 teaspoon cinnamon
1/2 teaspoon ground cloves

2 medium mixing bowls
7 small loaf pans or 4 medium loaf pans

Baking Time: 45 minutes to 1 hour 15 minutes
Baking Temperature: 350°

Preheat oven to 350°. Grease and lightly flour loaf pans. In a medium mixing bowl, cream shortening and sugar; add eggs, pumpkin and water. Sift in dry ingredients. Bake for 45 minutes to 1 hour 15 minutes, depending upon your oven and the size and amount of pans. Insert a toothpick to test for doneness.

Honey and Nut Cream Cheese Icing:
1/2 cup butter
1 teaspoon vanilla
1 package (8 ounces) regular cream cheese
1/4 cup honey (you may use more for thinner consistency)
1/2 cup pecans, finely chopped

In a medium mixing bowl, mix all ingredients except nuts. Frost loaves, then sprinkle desired amount of pecans on top.

Holly Crossing Bed & Breakfast

304 South Saginaw Street
Holly, MI 48442
(248)634-7075
(800)556-2262
www.hollybandb.com
hollybandb@yahoo.com

Hosts: Dan & Bobbie Straub

Holly Crossing is a Queen Anne Victorian, circa 1892, built in the turn of the century where the railroad tracks met Main Street in this historic railroad village. You will go back in time when you visit Holly's ornate Victorian shop fronts, feel the cobblestone underfoot and hear the sound of a train whistle. Holly Crossing offers six unique rooms, all with queen beds, private baths, four with jet tubs and three with fireplaces. Our rooms are decorated with antiques, special touches and amenities to make your romantic stay as cozy as home. Holly Crossing is within walking distance of shopping and several restaurants. Holly also offers two state parks, golfing, canoeing, skiing, horseback riding, two beaches, and hot air ballooning. Or you can choose to just relax in the garden gazebo next to the water garden with its soothing sounds. You will enjoy a leisurely full gourmet breakfast with china, crystal, fresh flowers, candlelight and complimentary house baked goods available all day long.

Rates at Holly Crossing Bed & Breakfast range from $79 to $169.
Rates include a full breakfast.

Fruit Pizza

This easy-to-make recipe is delicious any time of year. Your guests will rave!

Serves 8-10

Dough:
1/2 cup (1/4 pound) soft butter
1/4 cup brown sugar
1 cup all-purpose flour
1/4 cup quick cook rolled oats
1/4 cup finely chopped walnuts

Filling:
1 can (14 ounces) sweetened condensed milk
1/2 cup sour cream
1/4 cup lemon juice
1 teaspoon vanilla

4 cups thinly sliced fresh fruit (such as kiwis, strawberries, bananas, peaches)

Glaze:
1/2 cup apricot preserves
2 Tablespoons brandy

1 small mixing bowl
1 medium mixing bowl
mixer
small saucepan
pizza or tart pan

Baking Time: 10-12 minutes
Baking Temperature: 375°

Dough:

Preheat oven to 375°. In a medium mixing bowl, beat butter and sugar until fluffy. Mix in flour, rolled oats and walnuts. Place dough on lightly oiled pizza pan and press into circle, forming a rim around edge. Prick dough with a fork. Bake for 10-12 minutes. Cool.

Filling:

In a small mixing bowl, mix milk, sour cream, lemon juice and vanilla. Refrigerate for at least 30 minutes. Spoon chilled filling over cooled crust. Arrange the fruit slices in a circular pattern over the filling.

Glaze:

Melt apricot preserves in a small saucepan over low heat. Add the brandy and mix. Strain. Brush the apricot glaze over the fruit.

Cover and refrigerate for 60 minutes. Cut into wedges and serve cold.

Sheridan on the Lake Bed & Breakfast

47026 Sheridan Place
Houghton, MI 49931
(906)482-7079
www.sheridanonthelake.com
bbriggs@chartermi.net

Hosts: Barbara & Bill Briggs

Our contemporary cedar shake home is nestled in pine, oak and birch trees on the shore of Portage Lake at the gateway to the Keweenaw Peninsula. Each room has a private deck overlooking the lake, cable TV, VCR, air conditioning, sitting area and private bath. Our Bed & Breakfast also features a full breakfast and Finnish sauna. A walking and biking trail is right outside the front door, and a golf course is nearby. Garden smoking is available; no pets, please.

Rates at Sheridan on the Lake Bed & Breakfast range from $99 to $129.
Rates include a full breakfast.

Fresh Corn Bacon Quiche

I serve this quiche often, and it is our most requested recipe. It is quick to make and very simple.

Serves 6

1 deep dish frozen piecrust, thawed (or equivalent)
3 large eggs
1/4 cup green onion, chopped
1 Tablespoon sugar
1 Tablespoon flour
1 teaspoon salt
1-1/3 cups half-and-half
3 Tablespoons butter, melted
2 cups fresh corn kernels (cut from 2 ears) or frozen corn, thawed
1/3 cup bacon bits or equal amount of cooked bacon, crumbled

1 pie pan
electric mixer
1 medium mixing bowl

Baking Time: 50 minutes
Baking Temperature: 425°

Preheat oven to 425°. Bake piecrust for 3-5 minutes.

Combine eggs, onion, flour, salt and sugar in medium mixing bowl and beat with mixer until blended. Add half-and-half and butter to mixture; mix until blended.

Layer corn and bacon in piecrust. Pour the liquid mixture over corn. Bake until filling is slightly puffed and top is golden, about 50 minutes.

Cool slightly. Serve warm.

Hall House Bed & Breakfast

106 Thompson Street
Kalamazoo, MI 49006
(269)343-2500
(888)761-2525
www.hallhouse.com
innkeepers@hallhouse.com

Hosts: David & Cathy Griffith

Warm and inviting, Hall House is a distinctive city Inn. We are located in a National Historic District adjacent to the wooded hillside campus of Kalamazoo College, moments from Western Michigan University and downtown Kalamazoo.

Prominent contractor Henry L. Vander Horst built Hall House in 1923 as his personal residence. This Georgian Revival home features Detroit Pewabic tile, Italian marble steps, ceiling artwork and mahogany woodwork.

All rooms are large, have private baths, cable TV/VCR, telephones, bathrobes, air conditioning and comfortable beds for a good night's rest. Some have fireplaces and one has a Jacuzzi for two. Theater, restaurants, museums, golf and Kal-Haven trail are nearby. Make Hall House your home away from home, where warm hospitality awaits you.

Rates at Hall House Bed & Breakfast range from $89 to $180.
Rates include a full breakfast on weekends and continental plus weekdays.

Garden Baked Eggs

This is a great vegetarian entrée. Complement this dish with fresh fruit, muffins and juice. Your guests will walk away satisfied and full. Your choice of meat can easily be incorporated by serving it on the side.

Serves 4-6

1 Tablespoon butter
1/4 cup diced onion
1/4 cup diced green pepper
1/3 cup chopped broccoli
9 eggs
1/2 cup milk
1/2 cup sour cream (regular or lite)
1 teaspoon parsley
1 teaspoon dill weed
1/2 teaspoon salt
1/4 teaspoon pepper
1/4 cup diced canned mushrooms
1-1/2 cups frozen shredded hash brown potatoes, thawed
1 cup shredded mild Cheddar cheese

1 large mixing bowl
1 small microwave safe bowl
8" x 8" baking dish

Baking Time: 35-45 minutes
Baking Temperature: 325°

Preheat oven to 325°. Spray baking dish with nonstick cooking spray. Melt butter in baking dish in oven.

Mix onions, green pepper and broccoli in small bowl. Cover with plastic wrap and microwave for 1 minute.

Beat eggs with fork in large mixing bowl. Add milk, sour cream, parsley, dill, salt and pepper to eggs; whisk until creamy. Stir in microwaved veggies. Add mushrooms, hash browns and cheese.

Pour in baking dish. Bake for 35-45 minutes or until firm.

Royal Rose Bed & Breakfast

230 Arbutus Avenue
Manistique, MI 49854
(906)341-4886
www.royalrose-bnb.com
rrbnb@chartermi.net

Hosts: Gilbert & Rosemary Sablack

Experience the exceptional Royal Rose hospitality, where people come by choice, not by chance. This centennial Bed & Breakfast has the distinction of being a 3-time National Award Winner. Amenities include king and queen size beds, private baths, whirlpool tubs, fireplaces and air-conditioning. Enjoy the sunroom or relax on the deck. Savor the full breakfast that is elegantly served.

The Royal Rose Bed & Breakfast is within walking distance to downtown, the boardwalk and lighthouse. Nearby sites include Mackinac Island, Tahquamenon Falls, Pictured Rocks, Fayette State Park, Seul Choix Lighthouse, Big Spring and Seney National Wildlife Refuge.

Rates at Royal Rose Bed & Breakfast range from $85 to $120.
Rates include a full breakfast.

Apricot French Toast

Guests rave about this French Toast because it is different from the usual French Toast they've experienced. The cream in the recipe adds richness and flavor. I serve this with a clump of red and green grapes and strips of bacon or sausage.

Serves 4 (12 slices)

8 ounces cream cheese, softened
2 Tablespoons apricot preserves
1-1/2 teaspoons vanilla, divided
1/2 cup chopped walnuts
1 loaf unsliced French bread
4 eggs
1 cup whipping cream
1/2 teaspoon nutmeg

1 small mixing bowl
1 large mixing bowl
electric skillet or griddle
1 saucepan

Preheat griddle to 350°. In a small mixing bowl, beat together cream cheese, apricot preserves and 1 teaspoon vanilla until fluffy. Stir in walnuts and set aside.

Cut French bread into 12 slices that are 1-1/4" thick. Cut a pocket in each slice and fill with about 1-1/2 Tablespoons cream cheese mixture.

In a large mixing bowl, beat eggs, whipping cream, 1/2 teaspoon vanilla and nutmeg. Dip bread in egg mixture and cook on griddle until golden brown.

Topping:
1 cup apricot preserves
1/2 cup orange juice

Heat preserves and orange juice in saucepan until boiling. Drizzle over finished French Toast. Garnish with a strawberry.

Rose Hill Inn Bed & Breakfast

1110 Verona Road
Marshall, MI 49068
(269)789-1992
www.rose-hill-inn.com
rosehill@cablespeed.com

Hosts: Gerald & Carol Lehmann

The Rose Hill Inn is an elegant 1860 Victorian mansion, once home of the founder of the American Boy Scouts. Twelve foot ceilings, fireplaces and fine antiques combine to create a mood of tranquility and escape from the modern world.

Six guest rooms are decorated with 19th century style but feature contemporary luxuries like air conditioning, private baths, cable TV and internet access. Enjoy our three and a half acres of landscaped grounds with pool and tennis court.

Rates at Rose Hill Inn Bed & Breakfast range from $99 to $160.
Rates include a full breakfast.

Baked Caramel French Toast

This recipe is wonderful because it is delicious, easy to make and quite flexible. The number of servings can be increased or decreased and seasonal fruits can be added for variety. They're great served with pork sausages.

Serves 8

2/3 cup maple syrup
2/3 cup butter
1 cup brown sugar
8 eggs
1-1/2 teaspoons vanilla
16 slices Texas toast, crusts removed, day old if possible
2 cups milk
sliced peaches or apples (optional)

1 medium mixing bowl
9" x 13" nonstick baking pan
aluminum foil

Baking Time: 50-55 minutes
Baking Temperature: 350°

Combine syrup, butter and brown sugar in the baking pan over low heat. If fruit is to be used, arrange it in the bottom of the pan. Place bread over syrup mixture in 2 layers.

In a medium mixing bowl, beat together eggs, milk and vanilla. Pour egg mixture over bread. Cover pan with aluminum foil and refrigerate overnight.

Preheat oven to 350°. Bake uncovered for 50-55 minutes.

Serve by turning each serving upside down on plate. Sprinkle with powdered sugar.

Country Chalet & Edelweiss Haus

723 South Meridian Road
Mt. Pleasant, MI 48858
(989)772-9259
(877)878-9259
www.countrychalet.net
rcl9259@earthlink.net

Hosts: Ron & Carolyn Lutz

Receive a warm welcome at the Bavarian-style homes in a peaceful setting on twenty acres with hills, ponds and beautiful sunsets. Experience a touch of Europe, with flowers on the balcony and down-filled duvets. We are ten minutes from Mt. Pleasant, CMU, Soaring Eagle Casino, golfing, canoeing and cross-country skiing.

Rates at Country Chalet & Edelweiss Haus range from $69 to $99.
Rates include a full breakfast.

Amish Pancakes with Blueberry Topping

Some of our guests ask for these every time they return to our Bed & Breakfast. They are sweet and delightful with blueberries and topped with warm blueberry sauce or maple syrup. Try adding different fruit for a change.

Serves 4-6

Pancakes:
- **2-1/4 cups proofed sourdough**
- **1-1/2 cups flour**
- **1 Tablespoon sugar**
- **1 pinch salt**
- **1/2 teaspoon baking soda**
- **1 Tablespoon baking powder**
- **3/4 cup milk**
- **3 large eggs**
- **1/4 cup melted butter**
- **blueberries or other fruit to add to batter (optional)**

Hint: Roll blueberries in flour prior to adding to batter.

Proofed sourdough:
- **1 cup flour**
- **1 cup sugar**
- **1 cup milk**

Feed Amish Friendship Bread sourdough starter every 4-5 days with identical ingredients.

2-quart bowl
whisk or mixer
griddle
medium saucepan

In a 2-quart bowl, mix all ingredients except fruit with wire whisk or mixer until all ingredients are moistened. Add fruit (optional). Heat griddle to 375°. Spray with oil or melted butter. Drop 1/4 cup batter on to hot griddle. Turn when lightly browned, about 2 minutes.

Blueberry Topping:
- **2 cups blueberries**
- **1 cup water**
- **1/2 cup sugar or Splenda®**
- **2 Tablespoons cornstarch**

In a saucepan, mix ingredients well, then heat to boiling, stirring often, until slightly thickened, about 1-2 minutes. You may add 1 Tablespoon butter, if you wish. Serve warm as a topping for pancakes.

Port City Victorian Inn

1259 Lakeshore Drive
Muskegon, MI 49441
(231)759-0205
(800)274-3574
www.portcityinn.com
pcvicinn@gte.net

Hosts: Barb & Fred Schossau

Welcome! Come into our century-old 1877 elegant Victorian Queen Anne, located on the bluff of Muskegon Lake. This grand lady offers great hospitality and was nominated for two years in a row as "Best in the Midwest" by Inn Traveler. We offer five rooms, all with private baths, comfy terry robes, remote-controlled air conditioning, ceiling fans, TV/VCR, modems, and all of the best amenities.

Relax on our second floor pergola with a view of the century-old park, or enjoy the view of Lakeshore Yacht Harbor on front porch gliders. Wake up to the aroma of a sumptuous breakfast served in your room, in our elegant dining room, or in our enclosed sun porch. After breakfast, take the trolley service to Lake Michigan and to many fine restaurants. Enjoy antiquing, bike trails, several golf courses, our Cross Lake Ferry to Milwaukee, the Muskegon Winter Sports Complex with luge, cross-country skiing, and our many beautiful parks on Lake Michigan.

Look us up on our website, www.portcityinn.com.

Rates at Port City Victorian Inn range from $125 to $180.
Rates include a full breakfast.

Champagne Fruit

What a great, elegant way to serve fruit! Get ready for the ooh's and ahh's!

Serves 12

4 apples and/or pears, cored and cut
1/4 cup orange juice
2 Tablespoons lemon juice
4 cups assorted fresh fruits, such as grapes, peaches, berries, pineapple and kiwi
3 Tablespoons sugar
2 teaspoons finely shredded orange peel
1 bottle (187 ml) champagne
1/3 cup sliced almonds, toasted
garnish with mint leaves

1 large mixing bowl

In a large mixing bowl, combine apples and/or pears with orange juice and lemon juice; toss gently to prevent fruit from discoloring. Add remaining fruit, sugar and orange peel; toss again. Cover and refrigerate.

Just before serving, stir in chilled champagne and sprinkle with almonds. Garnish if desired.

Wake-Up Fruit Blend

Try this wake-up instead of just plain orange juice. It is a sunrise delight!

Serves 2

2 cups orange juice
2 8-ounce containers strawberry flavored yogurt
1 medium banana
1/2 teaspoon vanilla
yogurt and strawberries as garnish

blender

Combine all ingredients in blender until well blended. Garnish with a dollop of yogurt and strawberries. Serve immediately.

Inn at Crooked Lake

4407 US 31 North
Box 139
Oden, MI 49764
(231)439-9984
(877)644-3339
www.innatcrookedlake.com
Innatcrookedlake@aol.com

Hosts: Diane & Mark Hansell

The Inn at Crooked Lake is a beautifully restored 1906 lakeside cottage. Hardwood floors, fireplaces, luxurious linens, and an expansive view make the Inn the perfect place to relax and recharge. Five comfortable guest rooms are appointed with everything you'll need to make your getaway enjoyable. Our guests are pampered with our guest refreshment center, dessert, and our own blend of fresh-roasted coffee each evening and breakfast. Find out why our Inn is one of the top three Bed & Breakfasts in the Midwest as chosen by Midwest Living Magazine. Only five miles north of Petoskey and 25 miles south of Mackinac, we're right in the middle of Northern Michigan.

Rates at Inn at Crooked Lake range from $90 to $195.
Rates include a full breakfast.

Inn at Crooked Lake Pumpkin Pancakes

This is a fall favorite of our guests. It is like having pumpkin pie for breakfast!

Serves 4-6

1-3/4 cups flour
3 Tablespoons packed brown sugar
1 teaspoon baking powder
3/4 teaspoon salt
1 teaspoon pumpkin pie spice
1/2 teaspoon cinnamon
2 large or 3 medium eggs
1-1/2 cups buttermilk
1/2 teaspoon vanilla
1 can (15 ounces) pumpkin
butter to coat griddle

1 large mixing bowl
1 medium mixing bowl
whisk
griddle

In a large mixing bowl, mix together dry ingredients. In a medium mixing bowl, whisk eggs, buttermilk and vanilla until frothy. Whisk in pumpkin until combined. Pour wet mixture into dry ingredients. Whisk together. Mixture will be thick. Use small amounts of water to thin just before cooking. It will be a little thicker than normal pancake batter.

Heat griddle to 350°. When hot, brush with butter, then wipe with a paper towel to remove milk solids (or it will burn). Pour 1/2-cup size pancakes on griddle. They will not bubble as much as regular pancakes. When brown on one side (about 2 minutes), turn and brown the remaining side.

Serve with maple syrup.

The Canfield House

4138 Portage Point Drive
Onekama, MI 49675
(231)889-5756
(866)889-5756
www.thecanfieldhouse.com
jane-paul@thecanfieldhouse.com

Hosts: Jane & Paul Mueller

The Canfield House is the Inn with two lakes. Guests can enjoy 200 feet of private beach on Portage Lake or the miles of Lake Michigan beaches just a short distance from the Inn. Built in 1900 as the summer home of lumber baron Charles Canfield, guests will enjoy the luxuries of today amid the charm of yesteryear. Full, served gourmet breakfast, afternoon refreshments, use of kayaks and bikes are all included in the rates. Restore the balance to your busy life at this beautiful lakefront Bed & Breakfast.

Escape to the natural beauty, privacy and luxury that is The Canfield House.

Rates at The Canfield House range from $95 to $165.
Rates include a full breakfast.

Breakfast Brulee

Brulee isn't just for dessert anymore. This wonderful one is a breakfast favorite of our guests at The Canfield House.

Serves 8

1 pound (16 ounces) assorted summer fruits: raspberries, blackberries, strawberries, blueberries
6 cartons (15 ounces total) French Vanilla La Crème Mousse
8 Tablespoons raw brown sugar
Equal® or superfine white sugar

8 4-ounce ramekins

Baking Time: 2-3 minutes
Baking Temperature: Broil

Clean fruit. If using strawberries, cut them into smaller pieces. Sprinkle with Equal® or superfine white sugar to taste.

Divide fruit into 8 ramekins. Spoon mousse over fruit to cover completely. Top each ramekin with one Tablespoon raw brown sugar.

Broil for 2-3 minutes, until the sugar melts and begins to caramelize. Leave sit for a couple of minutes before serving.

The Candlewyck House Bed & Breakfast

438 East Lowell
P.O. Box 392
Pentwater, MI 49449-0392
(231)869-5967
www.candlewyckhouse.com
maryjoneidow@yahoo.com

Hosts: John & Mary Jo Neidow

The Candlewyck House is an unusual blend of colonial and contemporary American style. Our six romantic rooms offer more than enough amenities to spoil even the most experienced traveler. Guests especially enjoy our fireplace suites with mini kitchens and a flower filled patio, perfect for sipping early morning coffee or afternoon wine. A library of more than 1,000 volumes awaits those dedicated bibliophiles, and for action packed moments, there are over 300 videos to choose from. We invite you to join our table, and while partaking of our full country breakfast, enjoy stimulating conversation with your fellow travelers.

After more than 13 years of being innkeepers, we still look forward to each new season. Because we are only a short walk to our pristine Lake Michigan beach and a quaint boutique-filled downtown, our guests often park their cars and join us for a step back in time while visiting Historic Pentwater.

Rates at The Candlewyck House Bed & Breakfast range from $99 to $139.
Rates include a full breakfast.

Lemon Buttermilk Pudding Cake

We spend our winters in Florida now that we are older, and we have the best lemon tree in our yard. I often freeze extra juice and bring it back to Michigan so we can enjoy our lemons year round. I think this is the best pudding cake recipe, and it's easy to prepare.

Serves 6-8

1/3 cup fresh lemon juice
1 Tablespoon lemon peel
3 large eggs, separated
4 Tablespoons butter or margarine, melted
3/4 cup sugar or Splenda® baking sugar
1/4 cup all-purpose flour
1/8 teaspoon salt
1 cup buttermilk

1 small mixing bowl
1 large mixing bowl
mixer
8" x 8" glass or ceramic dish
9" x 13" metal baking dish

Baking Time: 40 minutes
Baking Temperature: 350°

Preheat oven to 350°. Grease glass pan. Grate 1 Tablespoon lemon peel and extract 1/3 cup juice from fresh lemons.

In a large mixing bowl, whisk buttermilk, egg yolks, melted butter, lemon peel and juice, and 1/2 cup sugar. Beat in flour and salt until blended. In a small mixing bowl, with mixer at high speed, beat egg whites until foamy. Gradually add in remaining 1/4 cup sugar until soft peaks form. With rubber spatula, gently fold egg whites into lemon mixture. Pour cake batter into prepared pan.

Place glass dish into metal baking dish and place on center rack in oven. Carefully pour boiling water into metal baking dish until water level reaches halfway up glass dish.

Bake for 40 minutes or until top is golden and set. (Batter will separate into cake and pudding layers.)

Transfer dish from pan to wire rack to cool for 10 minutes. Serve warm.

Note: We like to add fresh strawberries and whipped cream as garnish.

Hexagon House Bed & Breakfast

760 Sixth Street
P.O. Box 778
Pentwater, MI 49449
(231)869-4102
www.hexagonhouse.com
innkeepers@hexagonhouse.com

Hosts: Fred & Sue Brander

The Hexagon House Bed & Breakfast is a fully restored historic home located in the lakeshore village of Pentwater, just south of Ludington and only 40 minutes north of Muskegon. The house was originally built in 1870 and has had a uniquely rich history.

Relax while bird watching on our covered porches, or re-energize your spirit with an in-room massage by one of our three certified massage therapists. All of our rooms have private bathrooms and a TV with DVD player, and two of our rooms have electric fireplaces. The suite is located on the first floor and has its own private section of porch with a wicker swing. The suite also has its own TV with DVD player, refrigerator, and a Jacuzzi tub.

All of our guests enjoy our spacious grounds (almost 3 acres), perennial gardens, walks along the nearby beaches of Lake Michigan, shopping, and dining. We even have several bicycles you can borrow to "tour the town." Check our website often for our seasonal and last minute specials.

Come and see for yourself why so many of our guests say that their stay at the Hexagon House was one of their best vacations.

Rates at Hexagon House Bed & Breakfast range from $100 to $225.
Rates include a full breakfast.

Peach Schnapps Stuffed French Toast

If you love peaches, then this dish is for you! It's not too sweet and has a rich, full-bodied taste. This recipe has become a real "crowd pleaser" and it's easy to prepare!

Serves 8

Filling:
- 1/4 cup peach schnapps, divided
- 1-1/2 packages (8-ounce package) cream cheese
- 2 Tablespoons half-and-half (may substitute 2% or whole milk)

French Toast:
- 1 loaf French bread, cubed (approximately 8-10 cups)
- 2 cans (15 ounces) sliced peaches, divided – drain juice and set aside for Peach Sauce
- 12 large eggs
- 1/3 cup maple syrup
- 1/2 teaspoon cinnamon
- 1/4 teaspoon nutmeg
- 2 cups milk

1/4 cup confectioner's sugar, garnish, optional
Cool Whip or vanilla yogurt, garnish, optional

9" x 13" baking dish
1 large mixing bowl
2 small saucepans
1 medium or large saucepan

Baking Time: 1 hour
Baking Temperature: 325°

Peach Sauce:
- 1 cup peach juice
- 1 cup sugar
- 1/2 teaspoon cinnamon
- 1/4 teaspoon nutmeg
- 2 Tablespoons cornstarch
- 1 can (15 ounces) diced peaches
- remaining simmered peach schnapps
- 1 Tablespoon melted butter
- 1 Tablespoon lemon juice

Filling Preparation:

Pour peach schnapps in a small saucepan and simmer for 10-15 minutes, until alcohol is evaporated. In a separate small saucepan, combine milk and cream cheese; simmer until melted and smooth. Stir occasionally to prevent burning. Blend in 1-2 Tablespoons of the simmered peach schnapps to taste.

French Toast Preparation:

Place half of the French bread cubes in the bottom of the baking dish. Pour melted cream cheese filling evenly over the cubed bread. Spread 1 can drained, sliced peaches evenly over filling. Top with remaining bread cubes. In a large mixing bowl, combine eggs, maple syrup, spices and milk; whisk until thoroughly blended. Pour egg mixture over bread. Cover and refrigerate 8-10 hours or overnight.

Preheat oven to 325°. Before baking, cover dish with aluminum foil. Bake for 30 minutes, then remove foil. Bake for an additional 30 minutes or until top is light golden brown. While French Toast is baking, prepare the ingredients for the Peach Sauce (below). Let dish set for 5-10 minutes before serving. Cut into 8 equal portions. Dust each plate with confectioner's sugar before placing serving on plate. Top with 1/4 - 1/2 cup Peach Sauce, a dollop of Cool Whip or vanilla yogurt, and a slice of peach. Serve with link sausage and fresh fruit slices.

Peach Sauce Preparation:

In a small saucepan, combine peach juice, sugar, spices and cornstarch. Stir often until saucc thickens to a syrup consistency. Mix in melted butter and lemon juice. Blend well.

Another great recipe from Hexagon House Bed & Breakfast:

Oatmeal Crème Brulee

Many of our guests rave about this recipe, even those who claim they do not like oatmeal. This recipe is easy to prepare and elegant to serve!

Serves 6-8

2-1/4 cups old-fashioned oats, uncooked
1/3 cup turbinado sugar
3-1/3 cups nonfat milk
2 eggs or 1/2 cup egg substitute, lightly beaten
2 teaspoons vanilla
1/3 cup firmly packed brown sugar
raisins, optional
dried cranberries or cherries, optional
chopped walnuts, optional
nonstick cooking spray

8-inch square glass baking dish
1 large mixing bowl
1 medium mixing bowl

Baking Time: 40-45 minutes
Baking Temperature: 350°

Preheat oven to 350°. Spray baking dish with nonstick cooking spray. In a large mixing bowl, combine oats and sugar. In a medium mixing bowl, combine milk, eggs and vanilla; mix well. Add milk mixture to oats mixture; mix well. Pour into baking dish. Bake for 40-45 minutes or until center jiggles slightly. Place on cooling rack.

Sprinkle brown sugar evenly over top of oatmeal. Using the back of a spoon, gently spread sugar in a thin layer across entire surface of oatmeal. Return to oven; bake just until brown sugar melts, about 2-3 minutes. Set oven to broil. Broil 3 inches from heat source until sugar bubbles and browns slightly, 1-2 minutes.

Spoon into bowls. Sprinkle with raisins, dried cranberries or cherries and chopped walnuts and serve with milk, if desired. Garnish with a sprig of mint or a pad of butter. Serve with fresh baked muffins or breads and your choice of meat (bacon or link sausages).

Another great recipe from Hexagon House Bed & Breakfast:

Lemon Coffee Cake

This delicious, simple recipe will bring raves from your guests! Whenever you need a quick dessert for unexpected guests or a great dessert for a picnic, pull out this recipe!

Serves 8-10

1-1/4 cups sugar, divided
3/4 cup vegetable oil
4 eggs
2 cups flour
1 teaspoon baking powder
1/2 teaspoon salt
1 can (15 ounces) lemon pie filling
1-1/2 teaspoons cinnamon
nonstick cooking spray

2 large mixing bowls
1 small mixing bowl
13 x 9 x 2 inch baking dish

Baking Time: 30 minutes
Baking Temperature: 350°

Preheat oven to 350°. Grease baking dish with nonstick cooking spray. In a large mixing bowl, combine 1 cup sugar and oil; mix well. Add eggs and beat until light and lemon colored. In a separate large mixing bowl, combine flour, baking powder and salt. Add dry mixture to the egg mixture and mix well.

Pour half the batter into prepared baking dish. Spread pie filling over batter. Top with remaining batter. In a small mixing bowl, combine cinnamon and remaining sugar. Sprinkle sugar mixture over batter.

Bake for 30 minutes or until a toothpick inserted in the middle comes out clean.

Hill Estate

602 Lakeview Avenue
Port Huron, MI 48060
(810)982-8187
(877)982-8187
www.hillestatebandb.com

Hosts: Casey & Carrie Harris

Enjoy charming surroundings and warm hospitality at the Hill Estate. The Inn features three cozy and uniquely decorated rooms, each with its own private bath. We are located in a quiet, residential area close to fine restaurants, shopping and the sandy beaches of Lake Huron. One of the favorite activities of our guests is to watch the ships enter the St. Clair River. Full breakfast is served each morning.

Rates at Hill Estate range from $85 to $149.
Rates include a full breakfast.

Baked French Toast with Cherry Topping

A fantastic choice for breakfast when cherries are in season. Preparing (pitting) the fresh cherries can take a little extra time, but it is definitely time well spent! We've received nothing but rave reviews. Returning guests request this year after year.

Serves 4

French Toast:
- **1-1/2 cups milk**
- **6 eggs**
- **1/3 cup maple syrup**
- **2 Tablespoons sugar**
- **1 Tablespoon orange peel**
- **1/8 teaspoon salt**
- **8 slices French bread**

Cherry Topping:
- **4 cups fresh, pitted sweet cherries, halved**
- **1/2 cup orange juice**
- **1 Tablespoon sugar**
- **vanilla yogurt for garnish**

1 medium mixing bowl
1 large mixing bowl
2 9-inch square baking dishes
nonstick baking sheet
large spatula

Baking Time: 20-25 minutes
Baking Temperature: 400°

French Toast Preparation

In a large mixing bowl, combine milk, eggs, maple syrup, sugar, orange peel and salt. Pour half of the mixture into each of two square baking dishes. Dip both sides of each slice of bread in milk mixture. Arrange in the same baking dish. Cover with plastic wrap and refrigerate overnight.

French Toast Preparation

In a medium mixing bowl, marinate halved cherries in orange juice and sugar mixture. Marinate overnight in the refrigerator.

When ready to serve:

Remove cherry topping from refrigerator one hour before serving; topping has its best flavor when served at room temperature.

About one half hour before serving, preheat oven to 400°, with rack set in center of oven.

Carefully transfer the soaked French bread slices to a buttered baking sheet using a large spatula. Bake for 20-25 minutes or until golden brown. Turn slices over halfway through baking time.

Top each slice with 1/2 cup cherry topping and a dollop of vanilla yogurt.

Sage House Bed & Breakfast

829 Prospect Place
Port Huron, MI 48060
(810)984-2015
(866)585-0622
www.sagehouse.net
sagehouse@SBCglobal.net

Host: Joan Volker

Built in 1878, Sage House is a fine old Queen Ann style home on the north side of Pine Grove Park near the St. Clair River and Lake Huron. Albert Sage, conductor for the Grand Trunk Railroad, put plumbing in the house in 1890. He sold the house to Captain Alfred Chambers and his wife Clarissa in 1901, after the captain retired as commodore of the US Steel fleet. Now restored, you can sit on the porch and watch the boats or a ball game. Just a few of the many things that you can do during your visit include crossing the Blue Water Bridge into Canada or cruising the river on the Huron Lady or the tall ship Highlander Sea.

Rates at Sage House Bed & Breakfast range from $119 to $139.
Rates include a full breakfast.

Baked Spiced Apples with Ricotta Cheese Sauce

This apple is a picture of comfort on a cold winter's morning. The apples are all dressed up with cinnamon sticks, a warm mixture of maple syrup, ginger and butter drizzled over the top, and a dollop of Ricotta cheese on the side.

Makes 4 apples

4 medium Granny Smith apples, about 7 ounces each
4 Tablespoons butter
7 Tablespoons maple syrup
1/2 teaspoon ginger, freshly grated
4 cinnamon sticks

blender or food processor
9-inch pie plate
4 individual serving dishes

Baking Time: approx. 40 minutes
Baking Temperature: 450°

Preheat oven to 450°. Core apples to 1/3-inch from bottom; peel about 1-inch of skin from tops of apples. If needed, cut thin slice off bottom of apple to help them set upright on plate. Put apples in pie plate. Put 1/2 Tablespoon butter in each apple, followed by 1 Tablespoon maple syrup and 1/8 teaspoon ginger. Place remaining butter and maple syrup in bottom of plate.

Bake apples for 40 minutes, basting several times with pan juices. Place cinnamon sticks in apples for last 15 minutes of baking. Bake until apples are golden and tender (the skin may split). Transfer each apple on to an individual serving dish. Let baking juices stand until thickened, about 15 minutes.

Ricotta Cheese Sauce:
3/4 cup Ricotta cheese
2-1/2 Tablespoons confectioner's sugar
1/2 teaspoon ginger
1/4 teaspoon cinnamon
3 Tablespoons heavy cream

Puree Ricotta cheese, confectioner's sugar, ginger, cinnamon and heavy cream in a food processor or blender.

Serve a heaping Tablespoon of Ricotta Cheese Sauce with each apple. Drizzle with the warm syrup made from the baking juices.

South Cliff Inn Bed & Breakfast

1900 Lakeshore Drive
Saint Joseph, MI 49085
(269)983-4881
www.southcliffinn.com

Host: Bill Swisher

Overlook Lake Michigan at South Cliff Inn Bed & Breakfast, an English Country Style Bed & Breakfast. The exterior of the Inn is English Cottage Style with decks and perennial gardens overlooking Lake Michigan. The sunsets are beyond compare! The interior of the Inn is English Country Style with many beautiful antiques and imported fabrics. Each of the seven guest rooms is individually decorated and several of the rooms even have balconies that overlook Lake Michigan. All of the guest rooms have their own private bathroom, some with whirlpool tubs.

The atmosphere of the Inn is one of warmth and friendliness. The homemade breakfasts are created by the retired chef/owner and are an event that you will not want to miss. The Inn is located one mile south of the downtown area of St. Joseph, which has quaint shops, galleries, restaurants and entertainment.

South Cliff Inn Bed & Breakfast has received the sought after and honored award of "Readers' Choice Best Bed & Breakfast in Southwestern Michigan" for 8 years. South Cliff Inn was also cited as "One of 40 ways to pamper yourself" in Chicago Magazine. Midwest Living Magazine recognized South Cliff Inn as a "Good night's lodging you'll like along the way." The Inn has also been featured in the following publications: USA Today, The Herald Palladium, and The Other Side of the Lake. And, just recently, South Cliff Inn was featured on the Fine Living Channel on cable television. Finally, Great Lakes Getaways summed up everything by saying, "This is living! This is South Cliff Inn!"

We strive to make your stay at South Cliff Inn Bed & Breakfast a most enjoyable and relaxing experience.

Rates at South Cliff Inn Bed & Breakfast range from $85 to $225.
Rates include a full breakfast.

Country Breakfast Casserole

This is an old family recipe. It's great to make the day before and bake fresh in the morning. Everyone who tries this dish wants the recipe. Many of the recipes that I make are quite involved, so this is great to just pop in the oven while you are making other things.

Serves 12

14 slices white bread, crusts removed
5 Tablespoons unsalted butter, softened
1 pound smoked, cooked ham, chopped
2 cups grated Sharp Cheddar cheese
3 cups shredded Mozzarella cheese
6 eggs
2 cups milk
5 Tablespoons prepared mustard
3 teaspoons granulated garlic
1 teaspoon ground black pepper
nonstick cooking spray

2 medium mixing bowls
whisk
9" x 13" baking dish

Baking Time: 45 minutes plus 45 minutes
Baking Temperature: 350°

Spray baking dish with nonstick cooking spray. Butter bread on one side. Place 7 slices bread, buttered side down, in pan (cut 7th slice in half). Layer half of the ham then all of the Mozzarella cheese. Top with remaining bread slices, buttered side up. Spread remaining ham then Cheddar cheese.

In a medium mixing bowl, beat together remaining ingredients and pour over bread mixture. Make sure all is coated. Cover and refrigerate overnight.

In the morning, preheat oven to 350°. Remove cover and bake for 45 minutes. Remove from oven and spread topping (below) over top and bake for another 45 minutes. Let stand for 15 minutes before serving.

Topping:
1 can (10 3/4 ounces) cream of mushroom soup
1-1/2 cups sour cream
1 cup grated Sharp Cheddar cheese
1 can (8 ounces) sliced mushrooms, drained

In a medium mixing bowl, combine all ingredients while egg dish is baking.

Inn at the Park Bed & Breakfast

233 Dyckman Avenue
South Haven, MI 49090
(269)639-1776
(877)739-1776
www.innpark.com
info@innpark.com

Hosts: Bob & Jan Leksich and Marie Hudson

Guests delight in Victorian elegance and modern luxury at the Inn at the Park Bed & Breakfast. The nine sumptuous guest rooms are elegantly appointed with fireplaces, TV/VCR, private baths, and many have a soothing whirlpool bath. Awake from a good night's sleep to the aroma of our signature breakfast. Socialize in the evening over hors d'oeuvres. Stroll just one and one-half blocks to the beach to watch spectacular Lake Michigan sunsets. Our courteous and friendly staff is dedicated to helping you have an enjoyable and memorable visit to South Haven.

Rates at Inn at the Park Bed & Breakfast range from $90 to $235.
Rates include a full breakfast.

Havarti, Grape & Ham Kabobs

This easy, elegant recipe will add flair to any meal without a lot of effort. Your guests will rave!

Serves 8

1 cup white grape juice
1 Tablespoon fresh mint, chopped
1 Tablespoon lemon juice
16 seedless red and green grapes
16 cubes Havarti, Fontina or Provolone cheese, cut into 3/4" cubes
8 thin slices ham, turkey or prosciutto, fanned
1/2 cup balsamic vinegar

1-quart saucepan
2-quart saucepan
strainer
8 kabob skewers

Combine grape juice, mint and lemon juice in a 2-quart saucepan and bring to a boil. Remove from heat and let stand 5 minutes. Strain; discard mint. Add grapes and marinate 1 hour at room temperature or overnight in the refrigerator. Drain and discard marinate.

On a kabob skewer, alternate grapes, ham (fanned) and cheese.

In a 1-quart saucepan, heat balsamic vinegar over medium heat. Reduce the 1/2 cup vinegar to 1 Tablespoon and drizzle over kabobs.

Victoria Resort Bed & Breakfast

241 Oak Street
South Haven, MI 49090
(269)637-6414
(800)473-7376
www.victoriaresort.com
info@victoriaresort.com

Hosts: Bob & Jan Leksich

The Victoria Resort Bed & Breakfast reflects its historic beginnings while providing luxurious rooms with fireplaces and whirlpool tubs. We have the perfect combination of the friendly ambiance you expect from a Bed & Breakfast with the right amount of privacy for your getaway. At the end of our street are the sandy beaches of Lake Michigan, where you can catch a spectacular sunset any time of the year. Downtown South Haven is just a short walk down the tree-lined streets for excellent restaurants and great shopping. Whether you visit us in the chilly winter, hot summer sun or crisp fall, you'll find yourself planning another vacation to South Haven before you even leave the driveway!

Rates at Victoria Resort Bed & Breakfast range from $59 to $190.
Rates include a full breakfast.

Chocolate Chip Oatmeal Cookies

Our guests can't seem to get enough of these scrumptious oatmeal cookies. The cookie dough can be prepared ahead of time and frozen until ready to use. Just place the cookie balls on wax lined sheets, freeze for 30 minutes, then pack into freezer bags and leave in the freezer.

Makes 3 dozen cookies

1 cup butter, softened
3/4 cup brown sugar
1/2 cup sugar
1 egg
1-1/2 teaspoons vanilla
1 cup unsifted flour
1 teaspoon baking soda
1/2 teaspoon salt
1 teaspoon cinnamon
1/4 teaspoon nutmeg
3 cups oats, uncooked
2 cups semi-sweet chocolate chips
3/4 cup walnuts, coarsely chopped

measuring cups and spoons
1 medium mixing bowl
1 large mixing bowl
electric mixer
2 cookie sheets
wire racks

Baking Time: 11-13 minutes
Baking Temperature: 375°

Preheat oven to 375°. In a medium mixing bowl, cream butter, brown sugar and white sugar. Add in vanilla and egg. In a large mixing bowl, combine flour, baking soda, cinnamon, nutmeg and salt. Combine butter mixture into flour mixture. Stir in oats, chocolate chips and walnuts. Using hands, shape cookie dough into balls the size of golf balls. Place cookie balls 1-1/2" to 2" apart on cookie sheet. Bake for 11-13 minutes. Place on wire racks to cool.

Yelton Manor Bed & Breakfast

140 North Shore Drive
South Haven, MI 49090
(269)637-5220
www.yeltonmanor.com
elaine@yeltonmanor.com

Hosts: Robert & Elaine Herbert

The Yelton Manor Bed & Breakfast and The Manor Guest House grace the Lake Michigan beachfront site of the former Dewey Hotel, a popular tourist destination for over 100 years. On a lovely, landscaped corner in the charming resort town of South Haven, the two "Painted Lady" Victorian mansions were built to delight a new generation of inn-goers who desire luxurious lodging with all private baths, central heat and air conditioning, fireplaces and whirlpool tubs, balconies with lake views, fabulous homemade food, TV/VCR/DVDs, thousands of beautiful books, free movie library and spectacular award-winning gardens. Each house has porches, parlors, nooks and corners, affording each guest the opportunity for social interaction or personal, quiet escape. The Inn is also walkable to downtown shops, festivals, restaurants and harbors.

Seventeen gorgeous rooms are beautifully decorated and perfectly maintained at both The Manor and The Manor Guest House. The Manor is designed for the more traditional "social stay"; gourmet hors d'oeuvres are served each evening and a full, sit-down breakfast is enjoyed each morning. The Manor Guest House, on the other hand, is specifically designed to meet the expectations of guests preferring a more private getaway, and a lovely continental-style breakfast is delivered to the room each morning for private dining. No matter which style is chosen, all guests enjoy the loving service, lush gardens, famous treats like signature chocolate chip cookies and brownies, and luxurious accommodations.

The Yelton Manor was acclaimed "Top of the Crop in Luxury B&Bs" by the Chicago Tribune and in the "Top Ten B&Bs in the USA" by Amoco Motor Club in the '90s, then went on to win numerous prestigious awards through the decade, including InnTraveler Magazine's "Best Inn in the USA" distinction in 2004 and "#1 Lodging in Michigan 2004/2005" by TripAdvisor.com.

Rates at Yelton Manor Bed & Breakfast range from $100 to $290.
Rates include a full and continental breakfast.

Quiche Elaine

OK, so it's a little vain to name a recipe after one's self...but Elaine really did invent this and she's made it a zillion times, so we couldn't resist. Quiche is an ideal breakfast, brunch or even dinner dish. (We usually make these two or three at a time. You can easily reheat leftovers in the microwave, warming one slice at a time for about 45 seconds.) You can make your own crust, but we suggest that you make it easy on yourself, as we do: use frozen 9-inch pie shells. If you let them defrost slightly and pull the foil pan away gently, you can set the shell into a decorative baking dish and maintain the illusion that you made fresh pastry(!). This recipe is hearty, beautiful, and makes the house smell heavenly when it's baking.

Serves 4-6

1 frozen 9-inch pie shell, slightly defrosted
1/2 cup (4 ounces) diced raw chicken breast
3 Tablespoons slivered almonds
2/3 cup chopped broccoli
1/3 cup chopped carrots
1-1/2 cups grated Gruyere or Swiss cheese
3 eggs, slightly beaten
1-1/2 cups whole milk (2% milk is too runny)
3 Tablespoons grated Parmesan cheese
salt and pepper to taste

1 medium mixing bowl
cookie sheet

Baking Time: 30-35 minutes
Baking Temperature: 375°

Preheat oven to 375°. Place chicken, almonds, broccoli and carrots in bottom of pie shell. Sprinkle with Gruyere cheese.

In a medium mixing bowl, combine eggs, milk, salt and pepper. Pour egg mixture carefully over cheese. Sprinkle with Parmesan cheese.

Bake for 30-35 minutes. We always put a cookie sheet under the pie shell in the oven to catch overflow. (It saves on oven cleaning!) Allow to stand 10 minutes before slicing so that the quiche can "set up."

The Inn at Black Star Farms

10844 East Revold Road
Suttons Bay, MI 49682
(231)271-4970 ext. 150
www.blackstarfarms.com
Innkeeper@blackstarfarms.com

Hosts: Jill Ryan & Kari Merz

The sun is rising over Grand Traverse Bay. Horses are turned out to pasture and a rider sets out for the trails. The aroma of fresh baking rises from the Inn's breakfast room. A truck heads for the Creamery with milk for today's batch of Raclette cheese. The farm manager is in the vineyard checking on the progress of the grapes. These images reflect the slower pace of life you can experience at a special place: Black Star Farms.

Black Star Farms is a destination offering visitors a variety of distinctive choices, showcasing Leelanau Peninsula's rich heritage and agricultural abundance. World-class products and services, including premium vinifera wines and fruit brandies, hand-crafted cheese, luxurious all-season Bed & Breakfast Inn, championship equestrian facility and recreational trails, provide guests a full sensory experience.

Use Black Star Farms as a convenient base for your "up north" getaway. We are in the heart of the Leelanau Peninsula Vintners Wine Trail and close to quaint villages with superb restaurants, galleries and shops. Interlochen Center for the Arts, the Traverse Symphony Orchestra, live theater and local festivals all provide stimulus for your senses. Sleeping Bear Dunes National Lakeshore, golf courses, beaches and marinas, trail systems and winter sports areas make this the perfect spot for the recreational traveler in every season.

Rates at The Inn at Black Star Farms range from $150 to $375.
Rates include a full breakfast.

Black Star Farm Late Harvest Riesling Crepes
Filled with Leelanau Cheese Cherry Fromage

This is an impressive dish that can be made 1 or 2 days ahead of time. I like to serve it with sautéed Granny Smith apples and top it with our own maple syrup or Dornfelder grape reduction scented with cinnamon.

Serves 4

1/2 cup all-purpose flour
1/2 cup milk
1/4 cup Black Star Farms Late Harvest Riesling
2 eggs
2 Tablespoons melted butter
1-1/2 Tablespoons sugar
pinch of salt
1 container (8 ounces) Leelanau Cheese Cherry Fromage
1/2 cup clarified butter
nonstick cooking spray

stand or hand mixer
spatula
rubber spoon
3/4 ounce ladle
1 medium mixing bowl
baking dish
small saucepan
crepe pan
sauté pan

Baking Time: 5-7 minutes
Baking Temperature: 350°

Combine all ingredients in mixer except fromage and clarified butter. Mix until smooth. Heat crepe pan with clarified butter over medium heat. When pan is hot, ladle batter in pan. Starting on one side of pan, add batter and tilt the pan in a circular motion to coat bottom evenly; return to burner. After 45 seconds to 1 minute, flip crepe over and cook another 45 seconds to 1 minute. Turn out onto cooling surface, then repeat the process. Crepes can be made a day or two ahead of time. Yield - 12 crepes.

Sauce:
real maple syrup
or
2 cups Dornfelder grape juice
2 three-inch cinnamon sticks
1 large Granny Smith apple (optional)

If using syrup, heat before serving.

If making reduction, heat juice, add cinnamon sticks and reduce by half. Set aside. Peel, core, and slice apple and sauté in butter.

Preheat oven to 350°. Spread fromage evenly on precooked crepes; roll the crepes. Spray baking pan or sheet with nonstick cooking spray before placing crepes in pan. Bake for 5-7 minutes.

Place on plate. Pile with apples and ladle your choice of sauce. Garnish with berries, powdered sugar and mint sprig. Enjoy!

Aberdeen Stone Cottage

315 North Elmwood
Traverse City, MI 49684
(231)935-3715
www.aberdeenstonecottage.com
aberdeen@chartermi.net

Hosts: Bill & Bonnie Mathias

Enjoy the Grand Traverse region from this charming and convenient location. Find yourself steps away from bay front parks and beaches, within easy access to a bike trail system and minutes from downtown shopping and dining. Use Aberdeen Stone Cottage as a base to explore everything the city and environs have to offer—the celebratory bustle of the Cherry Festival, quiet days at the beach, or visits to area golf courses or ski slopes.

Rates at Aberdeen Stone Cottage range from $75 to $100.
Rates include a full breakfast.

Herb Garden Frittata

Return guests often request this favorite frittata recipe. We use fresh herbs from our own garden when in season.

Serves 4-6

1/4 cup olive oil or canola oil
3 small zucchini, thinly sliced
6 large eggs
1/2 teaspoon salt
1/2 teaspoon pepper
5 Tablespoons grated Asiago cheese (may substitute Romano or other hard cheese)
1 Tablespoon chopped parsley
4-5 basil leaves, cut in thin strips
1 Tablespoon chopped chives
1 tomato, thinly sliced
1 Tablespoon chopped oregano leaves, optional

1 medium mixing bowl
skillet

In a skillet, heat olive oil; add zucchini and brown lightly. Reduce heat and let zucchini cook down for 4-5 minutes.

In a medium mixing bowl, beat eggs, mix in salt and pepper, then add 4 Tablespoons cheese. Pour mixture into skillet and sprinkle with parsley, basil, chives and oregano. Cook the egg mixture over very low heat for about 20 minutes, until barely set.

Garnish with sliced tomato. Sprinkle with remaining cheese and place under broiler for 30-60 seconds.

Cut into wedges and serve with a garnish of fresh herb leaves.

Antiquities' Wellington Inn

230 Wellington Street
Traverse City, MI 49686
(231)922-9900
(877)968-9900
www.WellingtonInn.com
stay@WellingtonInn.com

Hosts: Barb & Hank Rishel

Antiquities' Wellington Inn is a 1905 neo-classical mansion located in the heart of Traverse City within the historic Boardman neighborhood. This spectacular home has recently been fully restored to its original grandeur and features period antiques throughout the nine guest rooms, dining room, library and living room. Two vintage 2-bedroom Carriage House apartments are offered for extended stays.

Each morning, guests are treated to a sumptuous full breakfast in the turn-of-the-century dining room. Refreshments and snacks are always available in the guest kitchen located off the third floor ballroom. This impeccably restored home offers all the modern conveniences of a small luxury hotel, including private baths, central air and wireless high-speed internet. It's an ideal venue for weddings, business retreats and special events. Luncheon teas and carriage rides are available by reservation.

This unique in-town neighborhood location is just 2 blocks from fine restaurants, shops, recreational trails and spectacular beaches. Gracious innkeepers will gladly help with any arrangements required to ensure a memorable stay.

Rates at Antiquities' Wellington Inn range from $170 to $250.
Rates include a full breakfast.

Crabmeat Frittata

This is an elegant yet quick and easily prepared breakfast entrée that will impress your most discriminating guest.

Serves 4

3 Tablespoons butter, divided
1/4 pound fresh mushrooms, sliced
2 green onions, cut into thin slices
8 eggs, separated
1/4 cup milk
1/4 teaspoon salt
1/2 teaspoon hot pepper sauce
1/2 pound lump crabmeat or imitation crabmeat, flaked and picked over to remove any shells
1/2 cup shredded Swiss cheese

2 large mixing bowls
electric mixer
10-inch ovenproof skillet

Baking Time: stovetop 5-8 minutes, then finish off under broiler
Baking Temperature: stovetop-medium, then broiler

Melt 2 Tablespoons butter in skillet over medium-high heat. Add mushrooms and onions; cook and stir 3-5 minutes or until vegetables are tender. Remove from skillet; set aside.

In a large mixing bowl, beat egg yolks with electric mixer at high speed until slightly thickened and lemon color. Stir in milk, salt and hot pepper sauce.

In another large mixing bowl, beat egg whites with electric mixer at high speed until foamy. Gradually add to egg yolk mixture, whisking just until blended.

Melt remaining butter in skillet. Pour egg mixture into skillet. Cook until eggs are set. Remove from heat.

Preheat broiler. Broil frittata 4-6 inches from heat until top is set. Top with crabmeat, mushroom mixture and cheese. Return frittata to broiler; broil until cheese is melted.

Garnish, if desired. Serve immediately.

The Union House Bed & Breakfast

16104 US Highway 12
Union, MI 49130
(269)641-9988
(866)468-9660
www.unionhousebb.com
unionhousebb@beanstalk.net

Hosts: Judy Scott & Barbara Wright

The Union House Bed & Breakfast is a 19th century Queen Anne Victorian farmhouse – a historic remnant of pioneer America built after the Civil War. Just a short distance from the Michigan-Indiana border, the Union House is located on US Highway 12, a major thoroughfare crossing Southern Michigan. This highway was formerly known as the Great Sauk Trail, extensively used by settlers and Native Americans traveling between Detroit and Chicago.

Guests enjoy the elegant beauty of European antiques, down comforters, memorabilia from every continent, rooms with private baths, and air-conditioning. There is a private guest parlor for socializing or enjoying TV, games and reading material from around the world. For guests interested in the great outdoors, we have 5 acres of wooded property with a nature path and secluded coves with benches. You can also browse through our gift shop to find a little memento of your visit.

Area attractions include Notre Dame University, Shipshewana – Amish Country, hundreds of lakes for fishing and boating, golf, and scores of antique shops. You will wake up to the aroma of homemade bread in the morning. A hearty, home-cooked full breakfast is served in the private guest dining room. Come relax, enjoy your stay with us, and experience "Life's Simple Pleasures".

Rates at the Union House Bed & Breakfast range from $75 to $95.
Rates include a full breakfast.

Chocolate Fudge Cake

A chocolate lover's dream! This is a decadent treat for those special occasions. It is especially good when served warm with vanilla ice cream or whipped cream.

Serves 12

1 box chocolate cake mix, any brand
1 cup hot coffee
1 cup light brown sugar
2 Tablespoons (heaping) unsweetened cocoa
10 ounces (1 package) miniature marshmallows
1 cup chopped walnuts

1 small mixing bowl
1 large mixing bowl
9"x13" cake pan

Baking Time: 30-40 minutes
Baking Temperature: 350°

Preheat oven to 350°. Spray pan with nonstick cooking spray. In a large mixing bowl, prepare cake mix, following the directions on the box, except substitute the water with cold coffee. Set batter aside.

In a small mixing bowl, mix hot coffee, brown sugar and cocoa. Pour mixture into cake pan. Pour marshmallows evenly on top of liquid mixture. Pour prepared cake batter over top of marshmallows (cover marshmallows thoroughly). Sprinkle nuts over top of cake batter.

Bake for 30-40 minutes. Cool in pan. Serve each piece upside down (fudge side up). Top with whipped cream or vanilla ice cream.

Note: You can cut the number of servings in half by simply cutting the ingredient portions in half and using an 8"x8" cake pan. Use a Jiffy Cake Mix for this halved recipe instead of a regular size cake mix.

Another great recipe from the Union House Bed & Breakfast:

Oriental Salad Dressing

A unique change of taste! This is especially good when served with chicken or seafood.

Serves 1-2

1/4 cup vegetable oil
3 Tablespoons rice vinegar
2 Tablespoons sugar
1 Tablespoon sesame seed oil
2 teaspoons soy sauce
1/2 teaspoon dry mustard

1 small mixing bowl or shaker

In a small mixing bowl or shaker, combine all ingredients and stir/shake well. Pour over crisp lettuce salad, toss and serve.

Suggestion: Add strips of grilled chicken breast and/or slices of water chestnuts to the salad.

Another great recipe from the Union House Bed & Breakfast:

Oven Baked French Toast

This simple, yet elegant recipe is an old-time favorite of many of our guests and friends. Serve with warm maple syrup, peanut butter or your favorite topping.

Serves 5-6

Nonstick cooking spray
4 eggs
1/3 cup honey
1 cup milk
1 teaspoon vanilla
1 teaspoon cinnamon
10-12 thick slices of day-old French or Italian bread
powdered sugar

shallow mixing bowl
cookie sheet

Baking Time: 20-25 minutes
Baking Temperature: 400°

In a shallow mixing bowl, beat together eggs, honey, milk, vanilla and cinnamon.

Dip bread into egg mixture, coating both sides thoroughly.

Place coated bread slices on cookie sheet. Pour any remaining egg mixture over top of bread slices. Cover with plastic wrap or foil and refrigerate for 2 to 24 hours.

When ready to bake, preheat oven to 400°. Uncover cookie sheet and bake for 20-25 minutes or until golden brown.

Sprinkle with powdered sugar.

Serve immediately with your favorite topping.

Cocoa Cottage Bed & Breakfast

223 South Mears Avenue
Whitehall, MI 49461
(231)893-0674
(800)204-7596
www.cocoacottage.com
relax@cocoacottage.com

Hosts: Larry Robertson & Lisa Tallarico

Larry and Lisa spent 10 years lovingly restoring their 1912 Arts and Crafts bungalow to its authentic splendor. Now open as the Cocoa Cottage Bed & Breakfast, we offer you quiet, refined character with world class attention to detail and personal touches.

You can relax by our cozy fireplace or on our sun-dappled screened porch. In summer, our elegant gardens invite you to just unwind. No matter the season, you will be treated to delicious chocolate indulgences and Larry's sumptuous award-winning breakfasts, named 2004 Best Breakfast in the Midwest and 2005 Best Breakfast in the USA.

Each room is uniquely furnished with Lisa's artistic touches, antiques and chocolate! All rooms have full private baths, queen/king pillow top mattresses, designer linens and toiletries, wireless internet and central air conditioning. Experience Lake Michigan's local beaches, White River Light Station, golfing, antiquing, shopping or any of our seasonal getaway packages. Open year round, we invite you to be our guest and share in our passion of the history and design integrity of the Cocoa Cottage Bed & Breakfast.

Rates at Cocoa Cottage Bed & Breakfast range from $139 to $179.
Rates include a gourmet full breakfast or organic light breakfast.

Chocolate Stuffed French Toast with Fresh Raspberry Sauce

What would you expect from a Bed & Breakfast with Cocoa in its name? Yes, chocolate is served with breakfast and we surprise our chocoholic guests with this requested favorite! Our guests love this chocolate surprise, especially with our fresh raspberry sauce, made from our home grown organic black raspberries. Each morning we also serve fresh strawberries with our Mama Tallarico's Classic Hot Fudge Sauce. So, even if we're serving our signature Cottage Eggs or Lemon Ricotta Pancakes, you are never far from a delicious chocolate fix at the Cocoa Cottage!

Serves 4-6

French Toast:

- **6 large eggs**
- **1 cup heavy cream**
- **2 teaspoons Grand Marnier**
- **3-4 Tablespoons unsalted butter, for griddle**
- **12 slices Pepperidge Farm Very Thin White Bread**
- **6 ounces fine quality bittersweet (not unsweetened) or semisweet chocolate, finely chopped**

Food processor
1 small mixing bowl
1 fine-mesh sieve
shallow dish
saucepan
heavy nonstick griddle
whisk

Raspberry Sauce:

- **4 cups (1 pound) fresh red or sweet black raspberries or 3-1/2 cups frozen raspberries, thawed**
- **1-1/2 Tablespoons fresh lemon juice**
- **1-1/2 cups confectioners sugar**

Purée raspberries, lemon juice and 3/4 cup confectioners sugar in a food processor. Sweeten with confectioners sugar to taste (up to 1/4 cup more). Force through a fine-mesh sieve into a bowl, discarding seeds. Can be made ahead and stored in refrigerator. Serve the sauce warm.

Garnish Options:
Confectioners sugar
Fresh raspberries
Fresh mint sprigs

Whisk together eggs, cream and Grand Marnier in a shallow dish until combined well.

Melt 1-1/2 Tablespoons butter on a griddle over moderately high heat. Dip 6 bread slices briefly in egg mixture until lightly soaked, turning once if necessary. Transfer to griddle, without crowding, and reduce heat to moderate. Lightly cook and turn over. Sprinkle 3 slices with 1 ounce chocolate and top with another slice of the lightly grilled toast. Press sandwiches gently with a spatula to help slices adhere. Cook, turning sandwiches over once, until chocolate is melted and French Toast is browned and cooked through, about 10 minutes total. Transfer to a plate and keep warm, covered. Wipe off griddle and make 3 more sandwiches in same manner.

Cut French Toast in half diagonally and serve with sauce and garnish. One sandwich per serving or 1-1/2 sandwiches for the hearty appetite. Enjoy!

White Swan Inn Bed & Breakfast

303 South Mears Avenue
Whitehall, MI 49461
(231)894-5169
(888)948-7926
www.whiteswaninn.com
info@whiteswaninn.com

Hosts: Cathy & Ron Russell

White Swan Inn is your destination for gracious hospitality, romance, relaxation and delicious breakfasts. Guests enjoy spacious and delightfully decorated bedrooms with private baths. The beautiful Cygnet Suite with its elegant whirlpool tub pampers the senses. A large screened porch filled with wicker furniture is the perfect spot to read a favorite novel or just watch the world go by.

The award-winning White Swan Inn is located in the wonderful resort area of White Lake, halfway between Chicago and Mackinac Island. The beauty of Lake Michigan with its sunsets and unspoiled beaches enhances the area; every season offers a variety of outdoor activities as well as theater, concerts and museums. The White Swan Inn is within walking distance of shops, dining and White Lake; bring your bikes for a trip on the paved Hart-Montague Bike Trail. Let us help you plan your next getaway with a special package combining lodging, food and a fun activity or event.

We appreciate our guests and you can be assured of always receiving award-winning service.

Rates at White Swan Inn Bed & Breakfast range from $99 to $169.
Rates include a full breakfast.

Asparagus and Red Pepper Tart

If you are looking for an easy but different entrée for breakfast, then here it is! No-fuss crust and fresh ingredients create an impressive treat for all your senses. Add a fresh fruit cup and a sweet muffin and your breakfast will be complete. Or, paired with a fresh salad, you have the makings for a delicious light dinner.

Serves 2-3

1/2 package (15-ounce package) refrigerated pie crust, room temperature
1 Tablespoon olive oil
1/2 pound asparagus, trimmed and cut into 1-inch pieces
1/2 cup chopped red pepper
1/4 cup chopped onion
1 teaspoon dried basil
2 ounces shredded Mozzarella cheese
2 ounces crumbled Feta cheese
2 Tablespoons Parmesan cheese
salt and pepper to taste

large skillet
baking sheet

Baking Time: 15 minutes plus 5 minutes
Baking Temperature: 400°

Preheat oven to 400°. In a large skillet, lightly sauté asparagus, red pepper and onion in olive oil; season with salt, pepper and basil. Unroll pie crust and place on ungreased baking sheet. Sprinkle Mozzarella cheese on pie crust within an inch of the edge. Spread cooked vegetable mix evenly on top of Mozzarella cheese. Top with Feta cheese. Fold edge of pie crust over vegetable/cheese mix. The crust will not completely cover vegetable mixture.

Bake for 15 minutes or until dough is lightly browned.

Remove from oven, sprinkle Parmesan cheese evenly over the crust and exposed vegetables and bake for 5 more minutes. Cool on wire rack for 5 minutes before serving.

Another great recipe from White Swan Inn Bed & Breakfast:

White Lake Blueberry Muffins

This is a guest-favorite muffin at the White Swan Inn. A hint of cinnamon adds a delicious accent. We are fortunate to have a local blueberry farm nearby for the freshest berries. While I don't have time to pick, I know that when I purchase berries in the afternoon, those same berries were picked that morning. I freeze large quantities of blueberries so that I can offer a summertime treat all year round. Note: If you freeze blueberries, do not wash them until you are ready to use them in your favorite recipes.

Makes 12-14 Muffins

2 cups all-purpose flour
1 cup sugar
2 teaspoons baking powder
1 teaspoon cinnamon
2 eggs, lightly beaten
1/2 cup butter or margarine, melted
1/2 cup milk
1/2 teaspoon vanilla
1-1/2 cups fresh or frozen blueberries

1 large mixing bowl
1 small mixing bowl
12-cup muffin tin

Baking Time: 19-22 minutes
Baking Temperature: 400°

Preheat oven to 400°. In a large mixing bowl, combine flour, sugar, baking powder and cinnamon. In a small mixing bowl, combine eggs, butter, milk and vanilla. Add wet mixture to dry mixture, stirring just until moistened. Gently fold in blueberries.

Fill greased or paper lined muffin cups 2/3 full. Bake for 19-22 minutes or until tops are golden brown. Remove to wire rack to cool.

Another great recipe from White Swan Inn Bed & Breakfast:

Overnight French Toast

We gets lots of rave reviews for this delicious French Toast. I have served this entrée at the White Swan Inn since we opened in 1995. Our guests love the flavor and the unique custard-like center.

Serves 6

1 loaf (1 pound) unsliced French bread
3 eggs
1/3 cup granulated sugar
2 cups milk
1 Tablespoon vanilla
vegetable oil for browning bread

1 large mixing bowl
9"x13" baking dish
1 large skillet
baking sheet

Baking Time: 15 minutes
Baking Temperature: 400°

Cut bread into 12 slices, about 1-inch thick. In a large mixing bowl, whisk together eggs, sugar, milk and vanilla. Dip bread slices into mixture, turning them once or twice until they are thoroughly soaked with liquid. Transfer slices to a baking dish as you work. Drizzle any remaining mixture over bread in baking dish. Cover dish with plastic wrap and refrigerate overnight.

Preheat oven to 400°. Heat a large skillet; add vegetable oil to pan to cover bottom. Place as many prepared bread slices as will fit in the hot skillet and cook them until the undersides are golden, about 3 minutes. Turn the slices and cook until second sides are lightly browned. Transfer slices to a baking sheet after they are browned.

Place baking sheet in oven until slices are cooked through and are puffed up, about 15 minutes. Don't overbake.

Serve hot with your favorite syrup.

Parish House Inn

103 South Huron Street
Ypsilanti, MI 48197
(734)480-4800
(800)480-4866
www.parishhouseinn.com
parishinn@aol.com

Host: Mrs. Chris Mason

Now with wireless internet service in all rooms, the Inn is one mile from Eastern Michigan University, five miles from Ann Arbor and twenty minutes from the Metro Detroit Airport at exit 183 on I-94. Complimentary cookies, tea, coffee, soft drinks and the video library are always available. Ypsilanti's Depot Town features the Auto Museum and the Fire Truck Museum plus shops, restaurants and parks, only a ten minute walk away. Originally the parsonage of the First Congregational Church built in 1893, it was totally restored in 1993 after a six-block move to its current location.

Rates at Parish House Inn range from $93 to $165.
Rates include a full breakfast.

Spicy Pears in Cranberry Sauce

The aroma of cinnamon and nutmeg mixed with the pears is tantalizing. It is very simple and can be made ahead of time.

Serves 8

1 can (16 ounces) whole cranberry sauce
1/2 cup sugar
1 Tablespoon fresh lemon juice
1/4 teaspoon ground ginger
1/4 teaspoon ground cinnamon
6 medium pears, peeled and quartered or sliced. Pears should be ripe.
vanilla yogurt as topping

9" x 13" glass baking dish
1-quart heavy saucepan
aluminum foil

Baking Time: 40-50 minutes
Baking Temperature: 350°

Preheat oven to 350°. Combine cranberry sauce, sugar, lemon juice, ginger and cinnamon in saucepan. Bring the mixture to a boil over medium heat, stirring often. Remove from heat.

Combine pears in baking dish with the cranberry mixture, stirring to coat pears. Cover dish with aluminum foil.

Bake for 40-50 minutes or until a fork pierces the pears easily. Chill in the refrigerator until ready to serve.

Serve pears with vanilla yogurt as a topping, either in individual sherbet dishes or in a large bowl.

Michigan Facts

Statehood: January 26, 1837; 26th state
State motto: If you seek a pleasant peninsula, look about you.
Origin of state's name: Based on Chippewa Indian word "meicigama" meaning "great water" and refers to the Great Lakes.
Longest suspension bridge: Mackinac Bridge (5 miles) connecting Upper and Lower Peninsula, opened Nov. 1, 1957

State Flower
In 1897, the **APPLE BLOSSOM** (*Pyrus coronaria*) was designated the state flower. Sponsors noted it was "one of the most fragrant and beautiful flowered species of apple." It is native to the state.

State Bird
In 1931, the **AMERICAN ROBIN** (*Turdus migratorius*) was chosen the state bird. It had been favored by the Michigan Audubon Society. Sponsors called the robin "the best known and best-loved of all the birds in the state of Michigan."

State Soil
In 1990, **KALKASKA SAND** was chosen as the state soil. First identified as a soil type in 1927, Kalkaska sand ranges in color from black to yellowish brown. It is one of more than 500 soils found in the state. Unique to Michigan, Kalkaska sand covers nearly a million acres in 29 Upper and Lower Peninsula counties.

State Stone
In 1965, the **PETOSKEY STONE** (*Hexagonaria pericarnata*) was adopted as the state stone. The Petoskey stone is fossilized coral that existed in the northern Lower Peninsula about 350 million years ago.

State Fish
In 1965, the **TROUT** was designated as the state fish. In 1988, the Michigan legislature specified the **BROOK TROUT** (*Salvelinus fontinalis*) as the state fish. The brook trout is native to Michigan and found throughout the state.

State Reptile
In 1995, the **PAINTED TURTLE** (*Chysemys picta*) was chosen as the state reptile after a group of Niles fifth graders discovered that Michigan did not have a state reptile.

State Fossil
In 2002, the **MASTODON** (*Mammut americanum*) became the state fossil. Fossils of the prehistoric mammal have been found in more than 250 locations in the state.

State Tree
In 1955, the towering **WHITE PINE** (*Pinus strobus*) was designated the state tree. It was chosen as a symbol of one of Michigan's greatest industries. From 1870 to the early 1900s,
Michigan led the nation in lumber production.

State Gem
In 1972, **CHLORASTROLITE** (literally "green star stone") was adopted as the state gem. Known as the Isle Royale greenstone, Chlorastrolite ranges in color from yellowgreen to almost black. It is primarily found in the Upper Peninsula.

State Wildflower
In 1998, the **DWARF LAKE IRIS** (*Iris lacustris*) was designated as the state wildflower. Native to the state, the endangered flower grows along the northern shorelines of Lakes Michigan and Huron.

State Game Mammal
In 1997, the **WHITE-TAILED DEER** (*Odocoileus virginianus*) was designated the state game mammal after the successful lobbying efforts of a group of Zeeland fourth graders. Found in every Michigan county, the white-tailed deer is an important natural and economic resource.

Innkeeper's Tips for Breakfast Preparation and Presentation

- Plan your meal with attention to color, textures and taste. Add something green (spinach, parsley, asparagus) and red (peppers, tomatoes, salsa) to the eggs. Chopped nuts and fresh berries add flavor and crunch to your muffins.
- Offer savory as well as sweet dishes to please all palates. Having a choice of cereals, granola, and yogurt on hand helps cover all bases.
- Make mornings easier by preparing as much as possible the night before: Set the table; chop fruit, pre-assemble the main dish so that it's ready to pop in the oven.
- Have containers of lettuce leaves and cherry tomatoes, or sliced oranges and grape clusters, at the ready for garnishes.
- Stock your pantry, fridge and freezer with ingredients you use often all prepped and ready to go, like chopped vegetables and herbs, grated cheese, crumbled bacon bits, and sliced mushrooms.
- A bowl of cut fresh seasonal fruit complements every dish and wins universal praise. Cantaloupe, strawberries, pineapple and blueberries, and kiwi makes up a rainbow of flavor and colors.
- For an attractive presentation, serve fruit chunks on skewers, or in champagne glasses, layered with yogurt.
- Stir the seasoning mixture into unsalted whipped butter for a tasty spread, or add it to olive oil for a dipping sauce.
- For a sweet spread, mix butter and/or cream cheese with honey, marmalade, preserves, and some orange zest.
- Lightly oiling your bread dough with cooking spray makes it easy to braid or mold.
- Using heavy cream in place of milk makes your quiche light and delicious – though decadent!
- A touch of lemon or orange juice will keep bananas, apples and pears from turning brown. Orange juice is less acidic.
- To enhance the flavor of pecans or walnuts, roast for 10 minutes on a cookie sheet in a 350-degree oven.
- Freeze blueberries, diced peppers and onions on a cookie sheet before transferring them to a zip-lock freezer bag, so that they don't stick together.
- Fill a shaker with powdered sugar to decorate French toast.
- For a versatile seasoning salt that livens up egg dishes, mix equal parts of dried parsley, garlic powder, onion powder, Italian seasoning, basil and salt.
- Use scissors instead of a knife to more easily cut parsley, chives and other herbs.
- Lettuce keeps longer if you refrigerate it dry, and wash just before using.
- A pineapple is sweet and ready to eat when the leaves at the very center pull out easily.
- Pre-bake your pie shells at 400 degrees for 7 – 8 minutes to eliminate soggy crusts.
- Freeze over-ripe bananas for future use in banana bread.
- Adding salt to the boiling water toughens fresh corn. Add sugar or honey instead.
- Can't remember which of your eggs are raw or hard-boiled? Spin them on the counter. Raw eggs wobble, while hard-cooked eggs spin like a top.
- When salting some foods, such as baked goods or scrambled eggs, use butter flavored popcorn salt. Because it is so finely ground, it disperses much more evenly, so you can actually use less salt. When making foods like scrambled eggs, it enriches with a buttery taste and allows you to use less butter when preparing them. It's much healthier when done that way!

Directory of Michigan Lake to Lake Bed & Breakfast Association Membership

Bold type: Inns listed in this book.

City	*Inn*	*Phone*	*E-mail Address*
Adrian	Briar Oaks Inn	517-263-7501	whitcherg@aol.com
Algonac	Linda's Lighthouse Inn	810-794-2992	lindasbnb@hotmail.com
Allegan	**Castle in the Country B&B**	**269-673-8054**	**castlebnb@chartermi.net**
	DeLano Inn B&B	269-686-0240	delanoinn@triton.net
	Montage B&B Inn	269-673-4105	mawarnerbb@charter.net
Alma	**Saravilla Bed & Breakfast**	**989-463-4078**	**ljdarrow@saravilla.com**
Ann Arbor	**Ann Arbor Bed & Breakfast**	**734-994-9100**	**pat@annarborbedandbreakfast.com**
Arcadia	**Arcadia House**	**231-889-4394**	**info@thearcadiahouse.com**
Auburn Hills	Cobblestone Manor	248-370-8000	stay@cobblestonemanor.com
AuTrain	Pinewood Lodge B&B	906-892-8300	pinewood@tds.net
Battle Creek	Greencrest Manor	269-962-8633	
Bay City	Angel's Lair B&B	989-893-6411	angelslairbnb@aol.com
	Clements Inn	989-894-4600	clementsinn@chartermi.net
	Keswick Manor	989-893-6598	keswickmanor@aol.com
Bay View	Gingerbread House	231-347-3538	mghouse@freeway.net
Beaver Island	Deerwood Lodge	231-448-3094	
Bellaire	Applesauce Inn B&B	231-533-6448	wendy@applesauceinn.com
	Bellaire Bed & Breakfast	231-533-6077	belbed@aol.com
	Grand Victorian Inn	**231-533-6111**	**innkeeper@grandvictorian.com**
	Stone Waters Inn... On the River	231-533-6131	stonewatersinn@torchlake.com
Beulah	Elliott House	231-882-7075	info1@elliotbb.com
Big Bay	Big Bay Lighthouse B&B and Spa	906-345-9957	keepers@bigbaylighthouse.com
	Thunder Bay Inn	906-345-9376	
Big Rapids	**Inn At The Rustic Gate**	**231-796-2328**	**ruticgate@starband.net**
Birch Run	Church Street Manor B&B	989-624-4500	owner@churchstreetmanor.com
Bois Blanc Island	Insel Haus	231-634-7393	
Boyne City	Deer Lake B&B	231-582-9039	info@deerlakebb.com
Brighton	Canterbury Chateau	810-516-2120	janv@ismi.net
Brooklyn	Chicago Street Inn B&B	517-592-3888	chiinn@aol.com
	Dewey Lake Manor	**517-467-7122**	**deweylk@frontiernet.net**
Burt Lake	Rohn House & Farm	231-548-3652	rohnhous@freeway.net
Carleton	Whispering Woods Bed and Breakfast	734-654-3111	nancyhubbell@hotmail.com
Central Lake	Bridgewalk B&B	231-544-8122	
	Moonkeeper B & B	231-544-3931	moonkeeper@torchlake
	Torch Lake Bed and Breakfast, LLC	**231-599-3400**	**info@torchlakebb.com**
Charlevoix	Aaron's Windy Hill Guest Lodge	231-547-2804	nancy@aaronswindyhill.com
	Charlevoix Country Inn	231-547-5134	cci@freeway.net
	Horton Creek Inn B&B	231-582-5373	babbitt@twin-valley.net
Chelsea	Chelsea House Victorian Inn	734-433-4663	innkeeper@chelseahouseinn.com
	Waterloo Gardens Bed & Breakfast	**734-433-1612**	**waterloogardens@prodigy.net**
Chesaning	Stone House Bed & Breakfast	989-845-4440	stonehousebnb@centurytel.net
Clare	**Gould Farm Bed & Breakfast Inn**	**989-386-3594**	**gouldfarm@hotmail.com**
Clark Lake	Claddagh B&B	517-768-1000	debmcfee@mindspring.com
Clarkston	Millpond Inn	248-620-6520	millpondbb@email.com
Clio	Cinnamon Stick Farm B&B	810-686-8391	cinstick@tir.com
Coldwater	Chicago Pike Inn	517-279-8744	
Coleman	**Buttonville Inn**	**989-465-9364**	**info@buttonvilleinn.com**

City	*Inn*	*Phone*	*E-mail Address*
Constantine	Inn at Constantine	269-435-3325	jan@innatconstantine.com
Douglas	Douglas House	269-857-1119	
East Lansing	Wild Goose Inn	517-333-3334	wildgooseinn@hotmail.com
East Tawas	**East Tawas Junction B&B & Guesthouse**	**989-362-8006**	**info@east-tawas.com**
Elk Rapids	Cairn House B&B	231-264-8994	hperez@cairnhouse.com
Ellsworth	**House on the Hill B&B**	**231-588-6304**	**innkeeper@thehouseonthehill.com**
Engadine	**Sandtown Farmhouse Bed & Breakfast**	**906-477-6163**	**tom@sandtownfarmhouse.com**
Fennville	Glenn Country Inn	269-227-3045	info@glenncountryinn.com
	Heritage Manor Inn	269-543-4384	rdhunter@heritagemanorinn.com
	Kingsley House	269-561-6425	innkeeper@kingsleyhouse.com
Frankenmuth	Bavarian Town Bed & Breakfast	989-652-8057	btbedb@juno.com
	Frankenmuth Bed & Breakfast	989-652-8897	BenderJB@Juno.com
Frankfort	Stonewall Inn	231-352-9299	stonewallinn@hotmail.com
Fremont	Sheridan House	231-924-5652	paula@thesheridanhouse.com
Fruitport	Village Park B&B	231-865-6289	mejeur@juno.com
Gaines	Sidebotham Inn	989-271-0331	mside@juno.com
Gladstone	Kipling House	906-428-1120	info@kiplinghouse.com
Glen Arbor	**Glen Arbor Bed & Breakfast and Cottages**	**231-334-6789**	**innkeeper@glenarborbnb.com**
	Sylvan Inn	231-334-4333	sylvaninn@earthlink.net
Grand Haven	Boyden House Bed & Breakfast	616-846-3538	boydenhouse@chartermi.net
	Looking Glass Inn	**616-842-7150**	**lookingglass@charter.net**
Grandville	**Prairieside Suites**	**616-538-9442**	**cheri@prairiesidesuites.com**
Grass Lake	A Place of Rest	517-522-4850	
Grayling	Flying Fish Lodge	989-348-7760	
	Hanson House Bed & Breakfast	989-348-6630	hansonhouse@voyager.net
	Twin Pine Lodge	989-344-9708	twinpinelodge@attglobal.net
Gulliver	Thistledowne at Seul Choix	906-283-3559	thistle@UP.net
Harbor Beach	State Street Inn	989-479-3388	info@thestatestreetinn.com
Harrison	Carriage House Inn	989-539-1300	innkeeper@carriagehouseinn.com
Harrisville	Copper Inn	989-724-7338	info@copperinn.com
Hart	Courtland Carriage House, B&B, LLC	231-873-3871	deanna@cchbb.com
Hartland	Farmstead B&B Ltd.	248-887-6086	
Hastings	Adrounie House B & B	269-945-0678	adtubs@mei.net
Holland	Dutch Colonial Inn	616-396-3664	dutchcolonialinn@juno.com
	Inn at Old Orchard Road	616-335-2525	orchardroad@chartermi.net
	Shaded Oaks B&B	**616-399-4194**	**shadedoaks@chartermi.net**
	Thistle Inn	616-399-0409	
Holly	**Holly Crossing B&B**	**248-634-7075**	**hollybandb@yahoo.com**
Houghton	**Sheridan On The Lake Bed and Breakfast**	**906-482-7079**	**bbriggs@chartermi.net**
Howell	Suite Dream' Inn	517-548-3948	stay@suitedreaminn.com
Imlay City	Das Lengemann Haus	810-724-9059	
Indian River	Kristin Place on Burt Lake	231-238-0200	nitro@racc2000.com
Interlochen	Hall Creek B&B	231-263-2560	
	Lake 'N Pines Lodge	231-275-6671	lake@2mm.com
Ithaca	Bon Accord Farm B&B	989-875-3136	bonaccordfarm@nethawk.com
Jackson	Rose Trellis Bed & Breakfast	517-787-2035	rosetrellis5@cs.com
Jones	Sanctuary at Wildwood	269-244-5910	info@sanctuaryatwildwood.com
Jonesville	Munro House B&B Health and Day Spa	517-849-9292	mike@munrohouse.com
Kalamazoo	**Hall House B&B**	**269-343-2500**	**thefoxes@hallhouse.com**
Lake Leelenau	Kirschbaum Hill B&B	231-256-0056	annemkirschbaum@aol.com
Lakeside	White Rabbit Inn	269-469-4620	info@whiterabbitinn.com
Laurium	Laurium Manor Inn	906-337-2549	innkeeper@laurium.info

City	Inn	Phone	E-mail Address
Leland	Aspen House	231-256-9724	info@aspenhouseleland.com
	Snowbird Inn	231-256-9773	stay@snowbirdinn.com
Lexington	Captain's Quarters Inn	810-359-2196	westwind@greatlakes.net
	Inn the Garden B&B	810-359-8966	innthega@greatlakes.net
	Powell House B&B	810-359-5533	
Lowell	McGee Homestead	616-897-8142	mcgeebb@iserv.net
Ludington	Abbey Lynn Inn B&B	231-845-7127	Abbeylynn@mishoreline.com
	Cartier Mansion	231-843-4435	
	Inn At Ludington	231-845-7055	innkreeper@inn-ludington.com
	Lamplighter B&B	231-843-9792	lamplighter@ludington-michigan.com
Mackinac Island	Bay View B&B	906-847-3295	BayviewBnB@aol.com
	Cottage Inn of Mackinac	906-847-4000	info@cottageinnofmackinac.com
	Haan's 1830 Inn	906-847-6244	
	Metivier Inn	906-847-6234	metinn@light-house.com
Mackinaw City	Deer Head Inn	231-436-3337	info@deerhead.com
Manistique	**Royal Rose Bed & Breakfast**	**906-341-4886**	**rrbnb@chartermi.net**
Marine City	Heather House	810-765-3175	
Marshall	National House Inn	269-781-7374	innkeeper@NHI.com
	Olde Farmhouse B&B	269-789-2349	theoldefarmhouse@core.com
	Rose Hill Inn	**269-789-1992**	**rosehillinnkeeper@cablespeed.com**
Mio	Teaspoon B&B	989-826-3889	stay@teaspoonbb.com
Monroe	Lotus Bed and Breakfast	734-735-1077	lotusbnb@aol.com
Mt. Pleasant	**Country Chalet/Edelweiss Haus**	**989-772-9259**	**RCL9259@earthlink.net**
Muskegon	Hackley-Holt House B&B	231-725-7303	mlarchambault@yahoo.com
	Langeland House	231-728-9404	ebsnflows.langeland@verizon.net
	Port City Victorian Inn	**231-759-0205**	**pcvicinn@gte.net**
National City	Good Tour Bed and Breakfast	989-362-7047	
Newberry	MacLeod House	906-293-3841	fcicala@up.net
North Lakeport	Adventure Inn B&B	810-327-6513	stay@adventureinnbedandbreakfast.com
Northport	Days Gone By B&B	231-386-5114	jane@daysgonebybnb.com
	Old Mill Pond	231-386-7341	decompi@traverse.net
Oden	**Inn at Crooked Lake**	**231-439-9984**	**innatcrookedlake@aol.com**
Omena	A Place In Thyme	231-386-7006	aplaceinthyme@traverse.net
	Frieda's B & B	231-386-7274	
	Omena Sunset Lodge B & B	231-386-9080	
Onekama	**Canfield House**	**231-889-5756**	**jane-paul@thecanfieldhouse.com**
Oscoda	Huron House	989-739-9255	huron@huronhouse.com
	Manor House Inn	989-739-1977	manorhouseoscoda@aol.com
Pentwater	**Candlewyck House**	**231-869-5967**	**maryjoneidow@yahoo.com**
	Hexagon House B&B	**231-869-4102**	**staff@hexagonhouse.com**
	Historic Nickerson Inn	231-869-6731	nickerson@voyager.net
	Pentwater Abbey	231-869-4094	
Perry	Cobb House	517-625-7443	twillson@voyager.net
Petoskey	Serenity A Bed & Breakfast	231-347-6171	stay@serenitybb.com
	Terrace Inn	231-347-2410	info@theterraceinn.com
Pinckney	Bunn-Pher Hill Bed & Breakfast	734-878-9236	
Pleasant Lake	Hankerd Inn	517-769-6153	hankerd@voyager.net
Plymouth	932 Penniman - A Bed & Breakfast	734-414-7444	
Port Hope	Stafford House Bed & Breakfast	989-428-4554	staffordhouse@centurytel.net
Port Huron	**Hill Estate Bed & Breakfast**	**810-982-8187**	**hillestate@bwb.net**
	Sage House	**810.984.2015**	**sagehouse@sbcglobal.net**
Port Sanilac	Holland's Little House in the Country	810-622-9739	always@avci.net
	Raymond House Inn	810-622-8800	rayhouse@greatlakes.net

City	*Inn*	*Phone*	*E-mail Address*
Prudenville	Springbrook Inn	989-366-6347	info@springbrookinn.com
Romeo	Brabb House B&B	586-752-4726	stephens186@hotmail.com
Saint Clair	William Hopkins Manor	810-329-0188	whmanor@aol.com
Saint Ignace	Colonial House Inn	906-643-6900	chi@30below.com
Saint Joseph	Chestnut House B&B	269-983-7413	flcare@aol.com
	Riverbend Retreat B&B Inn	269-926-2220	info@riverbendretreatbb.com
	South Cliff Inn	**269-983-4881**	
Saugatuck	Birds of A Feather Inn	269-857-1955	teresadingman@yahoo.com
	Park House Inn	269-857-4535	
	Sherwood Forest B&B	269-857-1246	sf@sherwoodforestbandb.com
	Twin Gables Inn	269-857-4346	relax@twingablesinn.com
	Twin Oaks Inn	269-857-1600	twinoaks@sirus.com
Scottville	Carrier Ridge Lodge	231-757-4848	info@carrierridge.com
South Haven	A Country Place B&B	269-637-5523	acountryplace@cybersol.com
	Carriage House at the Harbor	269-639-2161	webform@carriagehouseharbor.com
	Inn at the Park Bed and Breakfast	**269-639-1776**	**innkeeper@innpark.com**
	Last Resort, A B&B Inn	269-637-8943	innlastresort@i2k.com
	Monroe Manor Inn B&B	269-637-6547	monroemanor@msn.com
	Sand Castle Inn	269-639-1110	innkeeper@thesandcastleinn.com
	Seymour House	269-227-3918	seymour@cybersol.com
	Victoria Resort B&B	**269-637-6414**	**info@victoriaresort.com**
	Yelton Manor Bed and Breakfast	**269-637-5220**	**elaine@yeltonmanor.com**
Spring Lake	Seascape B&B	616-842-8409	
Stanton	Hotel Montcalm Bed & Breakfast	989-831-5055	hotelmtc@pathwaynet.com
Stanwood	Outback Lodge & Stables	231-972-7255	outbacklodge@centurytel.net
Sturgis	Willow Glen Pond B&B	269-651-3291	willowglen@charter.net
Suttons Bay	**Inn at Black Star Farms**	**231-271-4970**	**innkeeper@blackstarfarms.com**
	Korner Kottage B&B	231-271-2711	info@kornerkottage.com
Traverse City	**Aberdeen Stone Cottage**	**231-935-3715**	**aberdeen@chartermi.net**
	Antiquities' Wellington Inn	**231-922-9900**	**stay@wellingtoninn.com**
	Bowers Harbor B&B	231-223-7869	verbanic11@aol.com
	Chateau Chantal	231-223-4110	wine@chateauchantal.com
	Country Hermitage B&B	231-938-5930	info@countryhermitage.com
	Field of Dreams Bed & Breakfast	231-223-7686	field@pentel.net
	Grey Hare Inn	231-947-2214	rabbit@greyhareinn.com
	Neahtawanta Inn	231-223-7315	inn@oldmission.com
	Petals n Pines B&B	231-223-4022	petalsnpines@aol.com
	Schooner Manitou	231-941-2000	tallship@traverse.com
Union	**Union House Bed and Breakfast**	**269-641-9988**	**unionhousebb@beanstalk.net**
Union Pier	Garden Grove B&B	269-469-6346	gardenbnb@triton.net
	Sandpiper Inn	269-469-1146	info@sandpiperinn.net
Vanderbilt	Hoods In the Woods B & B	231-549-2560	
West Branch	"LogHaven Bed, Breakfast & Barn"	989-685-3527	gotter@m33access.com
Whitehall	A Finch Nest	231-893-5323	afinchnest@chartermi.net
	Cocoa Cottage B&B	**231-893-0674**	**innkeeper@cocoacottage.com**
	White Swan Inn B&B	**231-894-5169**	**info@whiteswaninn.com**
Williamsburg	Yorkburg Manor B&B	231-267-5464	juyork@charter.net
Williamston	Topliff's Tara Bed and Breakfast	517-655-8860	info@topliffstara.com
Wyandotte	Bishop-Brighton B&B	734-284-7309	
Ypsilanti	**Parish House Inn**	**734-480-4800**	**parishinn@aol.com**

Index of Recipes

To order additional copies of
Celebrate Breakfast-
A Cookbook & Travel Guide
as well as other books in the Bed & Breakfast series or for a FREE catalog contact The Guest Cottage Inc. Also, visit us online at www.theguestcottage.com

The Guest Cottage Inc.
dba Amherst Press

PO Box 848
Woodruff, WI 54568
voice: 800-333-8122
fax: 715-358-9456